Instructor's Resource Manual

to accompany

Financial Accounting

Eleventh Edition

Jan R. Williams
University of Tennessee—Knoxville

Susan F. Haka
Michigan State University

Mark S. Bettner
Bucknell University

Robert F. Meigs
San Diego State University

Prepared by
Alice Sineath
Forsyth Tech Community College

McGraw-Hill Irwin

Boston   Burr Ridge, IL   Dubuque, IA   Madison, WI   New York   San Francisco   St. Louis
Bangkok   Bogotá   Caracas   Kuala Lumpur   Lisbon   London   Madrid   Mexico City
Milan   Montreal   New Delhi   Santiago   Seoul   Singapore   Sydney   Taipei   Toronto

McGraw-Hill Irwin

Instructor's Resource Manual to accompany
FINANCIAL ACCOUNTING
Williams, Haka, Bettner, and Meigs

Published by McGraw-Hill/Irwin, an imprint of the McGraw-Hill Companies, Inc., 1221 Avenue of the Americas, New York, NY 10020. Copyright © 2003, 2001, 1998, 1995, 1992, 1989, 1987, 1986, 1983, 1979, 1975, 1970 by the McGraw-Hill Companies, Inc. All rights reserved.

1 2 3 4 5 6 7 8 9 0 QSR/QSR 0 9 8 7 6 5 4 3 2

ISBN 0-07-252921-0

www.mhhe.com

Table of Contents
Williams/Haka/Bettner/Meigs
FINANCIAL ACCOUNTING, 11/e

This Instructor's Resource Manual contains three major parts. The first part, entitled Description of Learning Aids Included in the Text, introduces the various learning and teaching aids that accompany this edition. The second part, Assignment Suggestions, includes a sample assignment sheet and suggestions for condensing or expanding course content. The final section, Presentation Suggestions, is intended to provide instructors with assistance in presenting the text material on a chapter-by-chapter basis.

Description of the Text and Supplements

The eleventh edition of *Financial Accounting* includes more teaching and learning aids than an instructor can use in any given semester. In this first section of the Instructor's Resource Manual, we briefly describe these aids so that you may see which ones are appropriate for your course.

Assignment Suggestions

We recognize the difficulty in preparing an assignment schedule from a new or an extensively revised textbook. Therefore, the second portion of the Instructor's Resource Manual offers a sample assignment sheet. We also offer suggestions for condensing or expanding this suggested coverage.

Presentation Suggestions

We realize that it takes some time and effort to become familiar with the new edition of a textbook even if you have taught from the prior edition. What changes have been made in chapter content? Are there new illustrations and examples in the text? What about the problem material? Are your "old favorites" still there? Which new problems best illustrate the points that you want to emphasize? In the Presentation Suggestions section of this Manual, we try to pass on to other instructors our intimate familiarity with this twelfth edition of Financial Accounting. For each chapter we have prepared Chapter Summary, a restatement of Learning Objectives, a Brief Topical Outline, a daily breakdown of Topical Coverage and Suggested Assignment, a few personal Comments and Observations, some General Comments, some Supplementary Exercises, and an Assignment Manual summarizing the topical emphasis of the exercises and problems. We have also included the 10-Minute Quizzes from our Test Bank for each chapter and the solutions.

Chapter Summaries

These summaries, written for the instructor, contain a brief statement of the content and major theme or themes of each chapter. They are intended to assist course preparation by making as clear as possible at a glance, what material we have chosen to include in the text.

Learning Objectives

For your convenience, the learning objectives for each chapter have been restated here.

Brief Topical Outlines

These outlines are designed to assist instructors in coordinating classroom discussions with the material covered in the textbook. We find that class time is simply too scarce to allow us to discuss all the topics and ideas introduced in the text. The Brief Topical Outlines identify those topics which we believe are sufficiently important to require some classroom discussion. Also shown in the outlines are the page numbers of examples and illustrations in the textbook, which may serve as useful supplements to these discussions.

Topical Coverage and Sample Assignment

This section of the Manual repeats the sample assignment for each chapter and coordinates the Brief Topical Outline with the number of meetings allocated to the chapter.

Comments and Observations

As do most instructors, we have our own ideas as to which topics should be emphasized in the principles course, and which should be downplayed. We have learned from experience which topics are the most troublesome for introductory students. As the authors of the problem material, we know that certain problems or exercises are particularly well-suited to demonstrating specific concepts, or to sparking classroom discussion. In the Comments and Observations section of this Manual, we offer our personal suggestions as to what topics to emphasize, and which exercises and problems we find most useful in making specific points. For the benefit of instructors familiar with the prior edition of this textbook, we also identify the areas of change in this twelfth edition.

Our Comments and Observations section begins with a section entitled "Teaching Objectives." These are the topics that we feel deserve special attention in the classroom. Let us briefly distinguish between these "Teaching Objectives" and the "Learning Objectives" set forth for students in the textbook. "Teaching Objectives" relate to the use of classroom time. Certain "Learning Objectives" may be grasped readily from the textbook and may not require emphasis in class. On the other hand, side excursions to make the study of accounting more lively and relevant may be a very productive use of classroom time. There is, of course, considerable overlap between "teaching" and "learning" objectives; however, we find the distinctions between the two to be worth recognizing in this Manual.

Let us emphasize that the Comments and Observations section of this Manual reflects only our personal preferences and teaching style. Teaching is a very personal thing; topical emphasis and teaching style rightly vary from one classroom to the next. We believe that each instructor should seek to personalize his or her course, with an approach that recognizes not only the goals and capabilities of the students, but also the interests and background of the instructor. An Instructor's Resource Manual will never substitute for an enthusiastic instructor.

Asides

In many chapters, our Comments and Observations section is concluded with an Aside. The Asides are intended to provide a bridge between the study of accounting and the "real world." Most of the Asides deal with interesting or unusual events in the business community that are indirectly related to topics discussed in the chapter.

Supplementary Exercises

These additions to our problem material are of a rather specialized nature. Each chapter is introduced with an appropriate selection from a Business Week article to provide context and emphasize the usefulness of accounting information. We have provided an exercise based on additional articles. Most will require the student to obtain and review the entire article, and some will require additional research. The requirements of all of these exercises emphasize interpretation of accounting information and involve relatively little, if any number crunching. Secondly, we have provided a Group Exercise for each chapter. These also have been written to emphasize the use of accounting information. They require additional research and in some instances classroom presentations. As a result, they are particularly appropriate for assignment to student groups. Finally, an additional Internet assignment is provided. Many of these have been coordinated to the Business Week exercise to provide an expanded research project.

10-Minute Quizzes

The Test Bank accompanying the text contains a number of short quizzes for each chapter. For your convenience, these have been repeated here along with the solutions to the quizzes.

Assignment Manual

These tables link each Exercise, Problem, Case, *Business Week* Assignment and Internet Assignment to the chapter learning objective(s) that they emphasize. Each assignment is also rated as Easy (E), Medium (M), or Strong (S), and a time estimate is provided for each.

Chapter Summary

Our financial reporting system has changed greatly over the past 50 years and will continue to change. The financial world is experiencing unparalleled challenges, such as globalization, deregulation, and the widespread use of the World Wide Web. In the midst of these changes is the accounting profession that must provide reliable and relevant information to users. This chapter introduces accounting to the student as the means of providing the information to support such decisions. Two broad types of accounting information, financial and internal are introduced and discussed. The production and communication of information within an accounting system is introduced at the outset of the chapter.

The focus then shifts to the various consumers of accounting information and the uses to which they put that information. External users are discussed first with the natural emphasis placed on the decision-making needs of investors and creditors. The needs of these users are summarized in terms of their interest in cash flow prospects. The financial accounting process communicates these prospects. The objectives of the reporting process are discussed in some detail leading to a definitional listing of the financial statements. This segment of the chapter concludes with an overview of the characteristics of externally reported accounting information.

The orientation of the chapter now shifts to decision-making by parties internal to an organization and how internal accounting supports these decisions. Internal users are very broadly defined as all employees of the organization. Employees are supported by the internal accounting information system in three ways. First, the internal accounting system assigns decision-making authority over the organization's resources to employees. Second, the internal accounting system provides the information required to make decisions regarding these resources. Finally, employee performance is regularly evaluated and rewarded based on information supplied by the internal accounting system. The characteristics of internal accounting information are discussed at length. This discussion makes the student aware of the distinctions between financial and internal accounting.

The main body of the chapter closes with a discussion of the sources of integrity of accounting information. We introduce institutional features that contribute to the integrity of the information including, accounting principles and standards, systems of internal control, and audits of financial information. The roles played by organizations such as the AICPA, IMA, IIA, and AAA are discussed. We close by emphasizing the critical importance of the competence, judgment, and ethical behavior of professional accountants.

A *Supplemental Topic* titled *CAREERS IN ACCOUNTING* ends the chapter with an overview of career opportunities offered by the accounting profession. Opportunities in public, management, and government accounting are surveyed, as are career paths in education. We take this opportunity to distinguish between accounting and bookkeeping and to explain the minimal role played by bookkeeping activities.

Learning Objectives

1. Discuss accounting as the language of business and the role of accounting information in making economic decisions.

2. Discuss the significance of accounting systems in generating reliable accounting information.

3. Explain the importance of financial accounting information for external parties – primarily investors and creditors – in terms of the objectives and the characteristics of that information.

4. Explain the importance of accounting information for internal parties – primarily management – in terms of the objectives and the characteristics of that information.

5. Discuss elements of the system of external and internal financial reporting that create integrity in the reported information.

6. Identify and discuss several professional accounting organizations that play important roles in preparing and communicating accounting information.

7. Discuss the importance of personal competence, professional judgment, and ethical behavior on the part of accounting professionals.

*8. Describe various career opportunities in accounting.

Brief Topical Outline

    A Accounting information: a means to an end
       1 Accounting from a user's perspective
       2 Types of accounting information
          a Financial accounting – see *Case in Point* (page **5**)
          b Managerial accounting
          c Tax accounting
    B Accounting systems
       1 Determining information needs
       2 The cost of producing accounting information
       3 Basic functions of an accounting system
       4 Who designs and installs accounting systems
    C Financial accounting information
       1 External users of accounting information
       2 Objectives of external financial reporting - see *Case in Point* (page **10**) and *Your Turn* (page **11**)
       3 Introduction to Financial Statements - see *Cash Effects* (page **13**)
       4 Characteristics of externally reported information
          a Financial reporting-a means
          b Financial reporting versus financial statements

        c   Historical in nature

        d   Inexact and approximate measures

        e   General-purpose assumption

        f   Usefulness enhanced via explanation

D   Internal accounting information

    1 Users of internal accounting information

    2 Objectives of internal accounting systems– see *Your Turn* (page **17**)

    3 Characteristics of internal accounting information

        a Importance of timeliness - see *Management Strategy and Financial Reporting* (page **17**) and *Case in Point* (page **18**)

        b Identity of decision maker

        c Oriented toward the future

        d Measures of efficiency and effectiveness

        e Internal accounting information - a means

E   Integrity of accounting information

    1 Institutional features

        a Standards for the preparation of accounting information

        b Financial Accounting Standards Board - see *Case in Point* (page **20**)

        c Securities and Exchange Commission

        d Internal control structure

        e Audits of financial statements (see *Case in Point* - page **21**)

    2 Professional organizations – AICPA, IMA, IIA, AAA

    3 Competence, judgment, and ethical behavior – see *Your Turn* (page **23**) and *A Second Look* (page **25**)

Supplemental Topic

F   Careers in accounting

    1 Public accounting

    2 Management accounting

        a Financial forecasting

        b Cost accounting

        c Internal auditing

    3 Governmental accounting

        a The GAO

        b The IRS

        c The SEC

    4 Accounting education

    5 What about bookkeeping?

    6 Accounting as a stepping-stone

Topical Coverage and Suggested assignment

Class Meetings On Chapter	Topical Outline Coverage	Homework Assignment (To Be Completed Prior to Class)				
		Discussion Questions	Exercises	Problems	Cases	Internet
1	A - C			n.a.	3	
2	D - F	5, 9, 15, 16	4, 5, 7, 9, 10, 12	n.a.	5	1

Comments and Observations

Teaching objectives for Chapter 1

Chapter 1 introduces students to the users of accounting information, both external and internal to the organization. The objectives and characteristics of externally reported and internal accounting information are explained and contrasted with one another. The sources of integrity of accounting information are explained. Career opportunities in accounting are also discussed. In the class meetings relating to this introductory chapter our primary teaching objectives are to:

1   Explain the nature and requirements of the course.

2   Impress upon students the importance of keeping up with the coursework and of completing homework assignments on a timely basis. Impress upon students accounting is cumulative knowledge subject; students lost in Chapter 1 will likely have trouble the rest of the semester.

3   Describe the general purpose of accounting and various uses of accounting information. Explain the focus of this course relative to other accounting courses.

4   Provide an overview of external financial reporting.

5   Explain the nature of internal accounting and the information needs of internal users of accounting information.

6   Discuss the factors responsible for assuring the integrity of accounting information.

7   Briefly describe some career opportunities in accounting and explain why an understanding of accounting is useful to people other than professional accountants.

New features in Chapter 1

- Accounting is introduced as a system of information for decision-making.

- Both financial and internal accounting are introduced in parallel fashion by discussing (1) users of the information (2) their objectives with regard to the information, (3) the integrity of the information, and (4) specific characteristics of the information.

Although Chapter 1 draws on material from prior editions, the theme and organization of the material are new. The chapter places significant emphasis on the users and uses of accounting information. Detailed explanations of both external and internal reporting are included. We have also included extensive discussion of the sources of integrity in the reporting process. Numerous *Your Turn* and *Case in Point* capsules have been included to give students the flavor of using accounting information from the outset.

General Comments

Getting started   During the first class meeting, we find it worthwhile to spend a few minutes acquainting the students with the textbook and its supplements, and explaining the nature of an accounting course. For example, we show students that the text contains check figures to the problems on the inside cover, and that a glossary of key terms, a self-test, and usually a Demonstration Problem (with solution) appear at the end of each chapter.

We give a brief demonstration of the proper use of columnar paper and explain that all homework problems should be prepared in pencil. If the partially filled-in working papers are used (which we recommend), we show the students the worksheet for an extensive problem so that they will appreciate the time savings inherent in this supplement. We also mention that all two-page foldout work sheets are located at the **back of the working paper booklet**. We also advise students of the availability of the **Study Guide,** which contains chapter summaries, objective questions, and exercises for each chapter. The answers to the questions and exercises appear following each chapter in the **Study Guide.**

It is the nature of accounting that new concepts tend to build upon those that have come before. Therefore, we place a high priority on impressing the students with the importance of getting right to work and of keeping up with the progress of the class. Our experience has shown repeatedly that students who get off to a slow start or who fall behind early in the course will have increasing difficulty as the course progresses. Therefore, we recommend assigning a heavy homework load immediately.

"Accounting" is much more than crunching numbers   In teaching accounting, it too often happens that all available class time is spent demonstrating mechanical techniques and solving quantitative problems. Many students, however, have very little understanding of the environment in which accounting information is developed and used. Without this understanding, the relevance of accounting procedures and computations may not be apparent.

We urge instructors to give appropriate classroom time to introducing this environment. We favor in-class reviews of assignments emphasizing the *use* and *interpretation* of accounting information. This is especially true of the *Your Turn* and *Case in Point* cases included within the main body of the text. In addition, those problems that involve well-known companies introduce elements of the business community with which the student is at least partially familiar.

We also encourage instructors to address the many *nonquantitative* aspects of accounting, such as the information needs of decision-makers, accounting theory, systems design, internal control, auditing, ethics, and issues involving professional judgment. If students are to really "learn accounting," these topics deserve attention in both the classroom and in the textbook. One of our major goals in this eleventh edition is to offer examples, text discussions, and assignment materials that better illustrate what accounting "is all about."

In covering Chapter 1, we like to provide students with an overview of both the external and internal reporting process. Exercises *3* and *10* provide a good framework for this discussion. We also like to discuss Case *1* in class. The Internet assignment for this chapter provides an excellent opportunity to introduce students to this important research tool that will be used throughout the text.

Supplemental Exercises

Business Week Exercise

See "Commentary: Earth to Dot-Com Accountants", *Business Week*, April 3, 2000. The article surveys questionable revenue recognition practices of a number of companies. At what group of external users is this revenue information being aimed? How are these external parties using the information? Chapter 1 introduces a number of organizations concerned with the integrity of accounting information. Which of these is mentioned in the article? Why is this organization concerned with revenue recognition practices?

Group Exercise

If the *Supplemental Topic* was discussed, have student groups interview senior accounting majors and/or graduate accounting students and report on the career options their student colleagues are investigating.

Internet Exercise

Access the Microsoft web page www.microsoft.com and choose *About Microsoft*. Click on *Investor Relations* and go to the Annual Report for 2001. In the *Discussion and Analysis* section, review the rate of growth of Microsoft revenues. How does Microsoft seem to be doing compared to the sales of other high tech products? Which Big-Five accounting firm audited Microsoft in 2001? What impression does the auditor's report convey?

10-MINUTE QUIZ

CHAPTER 1　　　　　**NAME**_____ **#**_____

10-MINUTE QUIZ A　　　**SECTION**_____

Indicate the best answer for each question in the space provided.

_____　**1**　The best definition of an accounting system is:
　　　　a　Journals, ledgers, and worksheets.
　　　　b　Manual or computer-based records used in developing information about an entity for use by managers and also persons outside the organization.
　　　　c　The personnel, procedures, devices, and records used by an entity to develop accounting information and communicate this information to decision makers.
　　　　d　The concepts, principles, and standards specifying the information which should be included in financial statements, and how that information should be presented.

_____　**2**　Suppose a number of your friends have organized a company to develop and sell a new software product. They have asked you to loan them $10,000 to help get the company started, and have promised to repay your $10,000 0plus 15% interest in one year. Of the following, which amount may be described as the return on your investment.
　　　　a　$10,000.
　　　　b　$1,500.
　　　　c　$11,500.
　　　　d　some other amount.

_____　**3**　Which of the following is generally not considered one of the general purpose financial statements issued by a corporation.
　　　　a　Income statement forecast for the coming year.
　　　　b　Balance sheet.
　　　　c　Statement of financial position.
　　　　d　Statement of cash flows.

_____　**4**　All of the following are characteristics of managerial accounting, *except*:
　　　　a　Reports are used primarily by insiders rather than by persons outside of the business entity.
　　　　b　Its purpose is to assist managers in planning and controlling business operations.
　　　　c　Information must be developed in conformity with generally accepted accounting principles or with income tax regulations.
　　　　d　Information may be tailored to assist in specific managerial decisions.

_____ **5** Of the following objectives of financial reporting, which is the most specific?

    a   Provide information useful in assessing amount, timing, and uncertainty of future cash flows.

    b   Provide information useful in making investment and credit decisions.

    c   Provide information about economic resources, claims to resources and changes in resources and claims.

    d   Provide information useful to help the enterprise achieve its goals, objectives, and mission.

Match the organizations on the left with the descriptions on the right. Each description should be used only once.

Organization

Description

_____ Financial Accounting Standards Board

a. Government agency that regulates financial reporting by publicly-held companies.

_____ Securities and Exchange Commission

b. International organization dedicated to the advancement of internal auditing.

_____ American Accounting Association

c. Private organization most directly involved in the development and issuance of accounting standards.

_____ Institute of Internal Auditors

d. Organization dedicated to the advancement of accounting education and research.

_____ American Institute of CPA's

e Organization most involved with the ethical conduct of the accountants working within a company.

_____ Institute of Management Accountants

f. Organization that develops formal standards for auditing in the United States.

_____ Internal Revenue Service

g. A government agency that handles income tax returns of individuals and businesses and performs an audit function to verify the data presented.

The following is a list of various characteristics of accounting information. In the space provided, identify each as a characteristic of either financial or managerial accounting information.

1.   The information is summarized in a set of statements distributed to the public.

2.   The information is historical in nature. It reports the results of events and transactions that have already occurred.

3.   The timeliness of the information is more critical than its completeness.

4.   To increase its usefulness to investors and creditors, the information is usually accompanied by explanations from management.

5.   The information is intended to be used for planning and control decisions.

CHAPTER 1   NAME_____ #_____

10-MINUTE QUIZ D   SECTION_____

Provide concise written answers to the following:

1. Investors and credits are interested in a company's ***"cash flow prospects."*** What two specific concerns of investors and creditors are summarized by the term ***"cash flow prospects?"***

2. List the three financial statements that are used to communicate financial accounting information to interested external parties.

3. Provide a brief example to illustrate that externally reported financial accounting information must be based in part on estimates, judgments, and assumptions.

4. Briefly explain how generally accepted accounting principles enhance the integrity of financial accounting information.

SOLUTIONS TO CHAPTER 1   10 MINUTE QUIZZES

QUIZ A
1   C
2   B
3   A
4   C
5   C

QUIZ B
Financial Accounting Standards Board   C
Securities and Exchange Commission   A
American Accounting Association   D
Institute of Internal Auditors   B
American Institute of CPA's   F
Institute of Management Accountants   E
Internal Revenue Service   G

QUIZ C
1   Financial
2   Financial
3   Management
4   Financial
5   Management

QUIZ D
1   Return of investment and return on investment.
2   Balance sheet (Statement of financial position)
     Income statement
     Statement of cash flows
3   To account for the use of long lived equipment estimates must be made of the lifetime and scrap value of that equipment.
4   Adherence to generally accepted accounting principles assures comparability of accounting information among organizations.

Assignment Guide to Chapter 1

	Exercises	Cases					Net
	1 - 16	1	2	3	4	5	1
Time estimate (in minutes)	<15	15	15	15	30	30	30
Difficulty rating	E	E	M	E	M	M	M
Learning objective:							
1. Discuss accounting as the language of business and the role of accounting information in making economic decisions.	1, 16						
2. Discuss the significance of accounting systems in generating reliable accounting information.				√			
3. Explain the importance of financial accounting information for external parties – primarily investors and creditors – in terms of the objectives and characteristics of that information.	2, 3, 6, 7, 9, 16		√			√	
4. Explain the importance of accounting information for internal parties – primarily management - in terms of the objectives and characteristics of that information.	2, 7, 9, 10						
5. Discuss elements of the system of external and internal financial reporting that create integrity in the reported information.	7, 12, 13, 16	√					
6. Identify and discuss several professional organizations that play important roles in preparing and communicating accounting information.	4, 5, 8, 11						√
7. Discuss the importance of personal competence, professional judgment, and ethical behavior on the part of accounting professionals.	7, 14				√	√	√
*8. Describe various career opportunities in accounting.	15						

Chapter Summary

Financial statements are the primary means of communicating financial information to users. Chapter 2 covers the income statement, balance sheet, and statement of cash flows.

Chapter 1 set forth the objectives of the financial reporting process, and offered the observation that these objectives are met in large part by a set of financial statements. In this chapter, we take up the task of introducing the balance sheet, income statement, and the statement of cash flows.

The presentation is organized around the accounting equation. The equation serves as the basis for elementary transaction analysis. A continuing illustration examines the impact of a number of simple transactions upon the balance sheet of a simple service business. Revenue and expense transactions have been included so that we might introduce the income statement and statement of cash flows at an elementary level. This in turn has provided the opportunity to discuss and illustrate statement articulation.

Before closing, the chapter emphasizes the importance of adequate disclosure regarding both financial and nonfinancial information, thereby reinforcing the Chapter 1 theme that the financial reporting process is broader than the financial statements.

The chapter also covers accounting principles dealing with asset valuation, as well as an introduction to forms of business organization.

Learning Objectives

1. Explain the nature and general purpose of financial statements.

2. Explain certain accounting principles that are important for an understanding of financial statements and how professional judgment by accountants may affect the application of those principles.

3. Demonstrate how certain business transactions affect the elements of the accounting equation: Assets = Liabilities + Owners' Equity.

4. Explain how the statement of financial position, often referred to as the balance sheet, is an expansion of the basic accounting equation.

5. Explain how the income statement reports an enterprise's financial performance for a period of time in terms of the relationship of revenues and expenses.

6. Explain how the statement of cash flows presents the change in cash for a period of time in terms of the company's operating, investing, and financing activities.

7. Explain important relationships among the statement of financial position, income statement, and statement of cash flows, and how these statements relate to each other.

8. Explain common forms of business organization – sole proprietorship, partnership, corporation – and demonstrate how they differ in terms of their presentation in the statement of financial position.

9. Discuss and illustrate the importance of nonfinancial information to supplement the information in the primary financial statements.

10. Discuss the importance of financial statements to a company and its investors and creditors and why management may take steps to improve the appearance of the company in its financial statements.

Brief topical outline

A Introduction to financial statements
B A starting point: statement of financial position
   1 The concept of the business entity
   2 Assets
      a The cost principle - see *Case in Point* (page **45**)
      b The going-concern assumption
      c The objectivity principle – see *Your Turn* (page **46**)
      d The stable-dollar assumption – see *Case in Point* (page **46**)
   3 Liabilities
   4 Owners' equity
      a Increases in owners' equity
      b Decreases in owners' equity
   5 The accounting equation
   6 The effects of business transactions (illustrated on pages **48- 53**) - see *Case in Point* (page **53**)
   7 Effects of these business transactions on the accounting equation (see *Your Turn* (page **54**)
C The income statement (illustrated on page **56**) – see *Case in Point* (page **56**)
D The statement of cash flows (illustrated on page **57**) – see *Case in Point* (page **58**)
E Relationships among financial statements – see *Your Turn* (page **59**) and *Cash Effects* (page **60**)
F Financial analysis
G Forms of business organization
   1 Sole proprietorships
   2 Partnerships
   3 Corporations
   4 Reporting ownership equity in the statement of financial position (illustrated on page **62**)

H The use of financial statements by outsiders
  1 The need for adequate disclosure
  2 Management's interest in financial statements – see *Management Strategy and Financial Reporting* (page **65**)

Topical coverage and suggested assignment

Class Meetings on Chapter	Topical Outline Coverage	Homework Assignment (To Be Completed Prior to Class)				
		Discussion Questions	Exercises	Problems	Cases	Internet
1	A - D	3, 4, 11, 16	1, 4, 6	1, 3, 6	1	
2	E - H	17, 23, 24	11, 12, 13	7, 8, 9	3	1

Comments and observations

Teaching objectives for Chapter 2

The chapter introduces technical material, including the balance sheet, income statement, statement of cash flows, several generally accepted accounting principles, the accounting equation, and the effects of business transactions upon assets, liabilities, and owners' equity.

Our objectives in presenting this chapter are:

1 Describe the nature of financial statements. Explain the role of *generally accepted accounting principles* in this process.

2 Illustrate and explain a *balance sheet.* Define the terms *assets, liabilities,* and *owners' equity*, and discuss the basic accounting principles relating to asset valuation. Discuss the uses and limitations of this financial statement.

3 Introduce the *accounting equation* and illustrate the effects of business transactions upon this equation and upon a balance sheet.

4 Introduce the *income statement*, emphasizing the nature of *revenues* and *expenses*.

5 Introduce the statement of *cash flows* and distinguish among *operating, investing,* and *financing* activities.

6 Explain and illustrate the concept of financial statement articulation.

7 Define proprietorship, partnership, and the corporation as forms of business organization, and illustrate the effect of the form of organization on the presentation of owners' equity in the financial statements.

8 Explain the importance of adequate disclosure.

New features in Chapter 2

Much of the material on the balance sheet and transactions analysis appeared in the introductory chapter of prior editions. This material has been complemented by new coverage of the income statement and statement of cash flows, and reorganized into a comprehensive introduction to financial statements. Introduction of the income statement and the SCF has also made it possible to add a discussion of statement articulation. The end-of-chapter material has been expanded with several new exercises and problems to deal with the income statement, the SCF, and statement articulation. Case 2 has also been extensively modified to reflect the expanded treatment of financial statements.

General comments

Introducing the financial statements Our overriding objective in this chapter is to introduce students to the balance sheet, income statement, and statement of cash flows. We find Problem *8* useful for this purpose. Exercise *1* defining assets and liabilities, stimulates student interest when discussed in class. Also, it is short enough that they can be discussed without having been assigned as homework. We also recommend Problem *9* or *10* for initiating a lively classroom discussion of many of the concepts introduced in this chapter.

In covering Chapter 2, we like to continue the overview of the financial reporting process begun in Chapter 1. Cases *2* and *6* provide a useful framework for this discussion, but there is not enough time for both of them. Therefore, we rotate these cases in and out of our assignment schedules. If Case *6* is discussed, it would be appropriate to explain, in simple terms, the meaning and significance of debt covenants, in order to cultivate student appreciation of the importance of the accounting issues in this case.

Have you considered using annual reports? One means of bringing the "real world" into the classroom is through the use of annual reports. At the beginning of the course, we suggest that students write to a publicly owned corporation and request a copy of its annual report. Most companies are willing to comply: the reports usually arrive in about 10 days. (Students should write to the Corporate Secretary; names and addresses of publicly owned corporations are available in most campus libraries.) Annual report information can also be obtained through the SEC's EDGAR database available on the Internet, or from individual company home pages.

We encourage students to review these reports throughout the course and to note any similarities and variations between their reports and the textbook treatment of various topics. These comparisons increase students' interest in the course, prompt interesting questions, and demonstrate the diversity, which exists in practice.

Any annual report works fine. In fact a diversity of reports sparks comparisons and discussions among students, and prevents one company from being asked to supply an unreasonable number of reports. The reports need not be current to be useful. Once obtained, they may be passed on to future students for at least several semesters.

An aside In discussing the valuation of assets in the balance sheet of a business, the text stresses the cost principle. Therefore, the statement is made that the balance sheet of a business does not show "how much the company is worth." A different standard prevails, however, in the preparation of personal financial statements for an individual. In an individual's personal balance sheet, generally accepted accounting principles require assets to be valued at estimated market values. In addition, the estimated income tax liability, which would result from selling the assets at these values also, is included in an individual's balance sheet. Thus, the owners' equity section of a personal balance sheet shows the individual's net worth.

Why have we not discussed personal financial statements in the text? The answer is that very few individuals prepare personal financial statements in conformity with generally accepted accounting principles. Most individual financial statements are prepared in conjunction with loan applications. In these cases, the lender usually supplies its own preprinted forms, which specify the lender's standards for the valuation of assets and liabilities. These standards often vary from generally accepted accounting principles. For example, most lenders do not ask a borrower to estimate the income tax liability, which would result from liquidating appreciated assets at their market values.

Supplemental Exercises

Business Week Exercise

In "Weighing the Balance Sheet", *Business Week*, April 1, 2002, the author states many companies levered up their balance sheets in the late '90s. Highly leveraged companies must generate sufficient cash flow to service their debt. What is meant by a highly leveraged company?

Group Exercise

In "Schilit's Guide to Accounting Shenanigans", *Business Week*, April 4, 2002, Howard Schilit states the first sign of financial trouble for a company is a dramatic fluctuation in key indicators such as cash flow, accounts receivable, or assets. Schilit states the rough percentage of each part of the business pie usually remains stable. When one part of the equation changes, that could be the first sign of trouble. Research the article and discuss Schilit's seven shenanigans.

Internet Exercise

Case 2-2 instructs students to perform an analysis of an annual report. Rather than obtaining the report from the library or other source, have students download an annual report from a company web site and use this to complete the Case. Many companies make their report available on their web site, and most of the sites are relatively easy to locate through a search engine.

This chapter briefly introduces the ***stable dollar assumption***. Students can become familiar with the impact of inflation on monetary valuations at www.westegg.com/inflation/. This site provides a calculator that allows a monetary amount in one year to be converted into an equivalent amount in a second year. Students might like to calculate what their tuition would have been in 1980 dollars or what their textbook would have cost in 1980. The site contains numerous links to pages devoted to inflation related topics. One of the most informative of these is http://woodrow.mpls.frb.fed.us/economy/calc/cpihome.html. After some time at these sites, you may begin to wonder if we abandoned FASB Statement 33 too soon.

CHAPTER 2   NAME_____ #_____

10-MINUTE QUIZ A   SECTION_____

Indicate the best answer for each question in the space provided.

_____ **1**   The financial statements of a business entity:
   a   Include the balance sheet, income statement, and income tax return.
   b   Provide information about the profitability and financial position of the company.
   c   Are the first step in the accounting process.
   d   Are prepared for a fee by the Financial Accounting Standards Board.

_____ **2**   A balance sheet is designed to show the financial position of an entity:
   a   At a single point in time.
   b   Over a period of time such as a year or quarter.
   c   At December 31 of the current year.
   d   At January 1 of the coming year.

_____ **3**   Accounts payable and notes payable are:
   a   Always less than the amount of cash a business owns.
   b   Creditors.
   c   Written promises to pay a certain amount, plus interest, at a definite future date.
   d   Liabilities.

_____ **4**   The balance sheet of Bock Designs includes the following items:

Accounts Receivable	Cash
Capital Stock	Accounts Payable
Equipment	Supplies
Notes Payable	Notes Receivable

   This list includes:
   a   Four assets and three liabilities.
   b   Five assets and three liabilities.
   c   Five assets and two liabilities.
   d   Six assets and two liabilities.

_____ **5**   An accounting entity may best be described as:
   a   An individual.
   b   A particular economic unit.
   c   A publicly owned corporation.
   d   Any corporation, regardless of size.

Presented below is the balance sheet for Bellville Family Dentistry on January 1 of the current year.

BELLVILLE FAMILY DENTISTRY
Balance Sheet
January 1, 20__

Assets		Liabilities & Stockholders' Equity	
Cash	$ 20,000	Liabilities:	
Accounts receivable	31,000	Accounts payable	$ 45,000
Land	190,000	Total liabilities	$ 45,000
Building	225,000	Stockholders' equity:	
Equipment	35,000	Capital stock	456,000
		Total liabilities and	
Total assets	$501,000	stockholders' equity	$501,000

During the first few days of January, the following transactions occurred:

Jan 3   The business borrowed $50,000 from the bank, giving a note payable due in 90 days.
     4   Additional capital stock was issued in exchange for $9,000 cash.
     4   Equipment was purchased for $19,000 on credit.
     5   The business collected $18,000 of its accounts receivable and paid off $33,000 of its accounts payable.

Indicate your answer to each of the following questions in the space provided.

_____ 1   On January 6, the liability for accounts payable is:
               a $31,000.   b $12,000.   c $64,000.   d $81,000.

_____ 2   On January 6, stockholders' equity amounts to:
               a $465,000.   b $546,000.   c $456,000.   D $447,000.

_____ 3   On January 6, the amount of cash owned by the business is:
               a $20,000.   b $64,000.   c $97,000.   d $55,000.

_____ 4   On January 6, accounts receivable amount to:
               a $31,000.   b $49,000.   c $13,000.   d $16,000.

_____ **5** On January 6, total assets of the business amount to:

      a $465,000.   **b** $64,000.   **c** $527,000.   **d** $546,000.

CHAPTER 2   NAME_____ #_____

10-MINUTE QUIZ C   SECTION_____

Presented below is the balance sheet for Bellville Family Dentistry on January 1 of the current year.

BELLVILLE FAMILY DENTISTRY
Balance Sheet
January 1, 20__

Assets		Liabilities & Stockholders' Equity	
Cash	$ 20,000	Liabilities:	
Accounts receivable	31,000	Accounts payable	$ 45,000
Land	190,000	Total liabilities	$ 45,000
Building	225,000	Stockholders' equity:	
Equipment	35,000	Capital stock	456,000
		Total liabilities and	
Total assets	$501,000	stockholders' equity	$501,000

During the first few days of January, the following transactions occurred:

Jan 2   Equipment was purchased for $24,000 on credit.
     2   The business collected $14,000 of its accounts receivable and paid off $25,000 of its accounts payable.
     3   The business borrowed $40,000 from the bank, giving a note payable due in 90 days.
     3   Additional capital stock was issued in exchange for $15,000 cash.

Complete the following balance sheet for Bellville Family Dentistry on January 4 of the current year.

BELLVILLE FAMILY DENTISTRY
Balance Sheet
January 4, 20__

Assets		Liabilities & Stockholders' Equity	
Cash	$	Liabilities:	
Accounts receivable		Notes payable	$
Land		Accounts payable	_____
Building		Total liabilities	$
Equipment		Stockholders' equity:	
		Capital stock	
		Total liabilities and	
Total assets	$_____	stockholders' equity	$_____

Complete the January 31, 20__, balance sheet of McKenzie Legal Services using the following information.

(1)   Stockholders' equity at January 1, 20__, included capital stock of $160,000.
(2)   The land and building were purchased by the business for a total price of $190,000 on January 25, 20__, from a company forced out of business. On January 31, an appraiser valued the property at $250,000.
(3)   Additional capital stock was issued in exchange for $20,000 cash.
(4)   Retained earnings at January 31, 20__, amounted to $27,400.

MCKENZIE LEGAL SERVICES
Balance Sheet
January 31, 20__

Assets		Liabilities & Stockholders' Equity		
Cash	$ 10,000	Liabilities:		
Accounts receivable		Notes payable	$	
Land	60,000	Accounts payable		12,600
Building		Total liabilities	$	
Equipment	15,000	Stockholders' equity:		
		Capital stock	$	
		Retained earnings	_____	_____
		Total liabilities and		
Total assets	$_____	stockholders' equity		$_____

SOLUTIONS TO CHAPTER 2   10-MINUTE QUIZZES

QUIZ A		QUIZ B	
1	B	1	A
2	A	2	A
3	D	3	B
4	C	4	C
5	B	5	D

QUIZ C

BELLVILLE FAMILY DENTISTRY
Balance Sheet
January 4, 20__

Assets		Liabilities & Stockholders' Equity	
Cash	$ 64,000^a	Liabilities:	
Accounts receivable	17,000^b	Notes payable	$ 40,000
Land	190,000	Accounts payable	44,000^c
Building	225,000	Total liabilities	$ 84,000
Equipment	59,000^e	Stockholders' equity:	
		Capital stock	471,000^d
		Total liabilities and	
Total assets	$555,000	stockholders' equity	$555,000

Computations

a $20,000 + $14,000 (A/R collected) - $25,000 (paid on A/P) + $40,000 (borrowed) + $15,000 (invested) = $64,000

b $31,000 - $14,000 collected = $17,000

c $45,000 + $24,000 (equipment purchased) - $25,000 (paid) = $44,000

d $456,000 + $15,000 additional investment = $471,000

e $35,000 + $24,000 purchased = $59,000

QUIZ D

MCKENZIE LEGAL SERVICES
Balance Sheet
January 31, 20__

Assets		Liabilities and Stockholders' equity		
Cash	$ 10,000	Liabilities:		
Accounts receivable	25,000[c]	Notes payable		$ 20,000[f]
Land	60,000	Accounts payable		12,600
Building	130,000[b]	Total liabilities		$ 32,600[e]
Equipment	15,000	Stockholders' equity:		
		Capital stock	$180,000[d]	
		Retained earnings	27,400	$207,400
		Total liabilities and		
Total assets	$240,000[a]	stockholders' equity		$240,000

Computations

a   Total assets must be equal to total liabilities & stockholders' equity of $240,000.

b $190,000 (cost of land and building) less $60,000 for land = $130,000 for building. (Appraised value of property ignored.)

c   Accounts receivable must be $25,000 to achieve total assets of $240,000.

d $160,000 (capital stock at January 1) plus $20,000 (additional investment).

e   Total liabilities must be $32,600 to achieve total liabilities & owners' equity of $240,000.

f   Notes payable must be $20,000 to achieve total liabilities of $32,600.

Assignment Guide to Chapter 2

	Exercises	Problems										Cases						Net
	1 - 17	1	2	3	4	5	6	7	8	9	10	1	2	3	4	5	6	1
Time estimate (in minutes)	<15	15	15	15	15	20	20	35	40	35	30	30	30	30	30	15	35	25
Difficulty rating	E	E	E	M	M	M	M	M	S	S	S	S	M	M	M	E	M	E
Learning Objectives:																		
1. Explain the nature and general purpose of financial statements.																		
2. Explain certain accounting principles that are important for an understanding of financial statements and how professional judgment by accountants may affect the application of those principles.	4, 10										√							
3. Demonstrate how certain business transactions affect the elements of the accounting equation: Assets = Liabilities + Owner's Equity.	1, 5, 6, 7		√	√	√			√										√
4. Explain how the statement of financial position, often referred to as the balance sheet, is an expansion of the basic accounting equation.	2, 3, 9, 17	√		√		√	√			√		√		√				√
5. Explain how the income statement reports an enterprise's financial performance for a period of time in terms of the relationship of revenues and expenses.	12, 13, 17, 18								√			√	√					
6. Explain how the statement of cash flows presents the change in cash for a period of time in terms of the company's operating, investing, and financing activities.	11, 14, 17							√	√				√		√		√	
7. Explain important relationships among the statement of financial position, income statement, and statement of cash flows, and how these statements relate to each other.	15							√	√				√		√			
8. Explain common forms of business ownership – sole proprietorship, partnership, and corporation – and demonstrate how they differ in terms of their presentation in the statement of financial position.	8									√								
9. Discuss and illustrate the importance of nonfinancial information to supplement the information in the primary financial statements.																√	√	
10. Discuss the importance of financial statements to a company and its investors and creditors and why management may take steps to improve the appearance of the company in its financial statements.	16															√	√	

Chapter Summary

Maintaining a set of accounting records is not optional for a business. The IRS requires businesses to maintain records that can be audited. In addition, a business that does not maintain adequate records will likely operate inefficiently.

The recording process lies at the foundation of the financial statements. This chapter presents a comprehensive introduction to the accounting cycle. Coverage includes debit and credit rules for both balance sheet and income statement accounts, recording transactions in the journal and posting to the ledger, and the preparation of the trial balance.

In addition to the mechanical aspects of the accounting cycle, the student is also confronted with several major concepts from accounting theory. Net income is introduced as an increase in owner's equity resulting from profitable operations. The nature of revenue and expense is explored in detail as is the realization and matching principles underlying accrual accounting.

The comprehensive coverage has resulted in a relatively lengthy chapter. However, use of the continuing illustration of Overnight Auto is intended to allow for a reasonably efficient presentation of this significant material. All of the transactions dealing with balance sheet accounts are repeated from Chapter 2. Although the revenue and expense transactions are new to this chapter, the exposure to the income statement and SCF in the previous chapter should also shorten the time needed to cover recording such transactions.

Learning Objectives

1. Identify the steps in the accounting cycle and discuss the role of accounting records in an organization.

2. Describe a ledger *account* and a ledger.

3. State the rules of *debit* and *credit* for balance sheet accounts.

4. Explain the double-entry system of accounting.

5. Explain the purpose of a *journal* and its relationship to the ledger.

6. Explain the nature of *net income, revenue*, and *expenses.*

7. Apply the *realization* and *matching* principles in recording revenue and expense.

8. Explain why revenues are recorded with credits and expenses are recorded with debits.

9. Prepare a *trial balance* and explain its uses and limitations.

10. Distinguish between accounting cycle procedures and the *knowledge* of accounting.

Brief topical outline

A The accounting cycle
   1 The role of accounting records
B The ledger
C The use of accounts
D Debit and credit entries
   1 Determining the balance of a T account - see *Your Turn* (page **92**)
   2 Debit balances in asset accounts
   3 Credit balances in liability and owners' equity accounts
   4 Concise statement of the debit and credit rules
   5 Double-entry accounting -- the equality of debits and credits
E Recording transactions in ledger accounts (illustrated on pages **93-96**)
F The journal
   1 Posting journal entries to the ledger accounts
      a Ledger accounts after posting
G What is net income?
   1 Retained earnings - see *Case in Point* (page **100**)
   2 The income statement: a preview
      a Income must be related to a specified period of time - see *Case in Point* (page **101**)
      b Accounting periods - see *Case in Point* (page **102**)
   3 Revenue
      a The realization principle: when to record revenue – see *Cash Effects* (page **102**)
   4 Expenses
      a The matching principle: when to record expenses – see *Cash Effects* (page **103**)
      b Expenditures benefiting more than one accounting period - see *Case in Point* (page **104**)
   5 The accrual basis of accounting - see *Case in Point* (page **104**)
   6 Debit and credit rules for revenues and expenses
H Dividends - see *Your Turn* (page **105**)
I Recording revenue and expense transactions (illustrated on pages **105 - 111**) - see *Your Turn* (page **110**)
   1 The journal - see *Management Strategy and Financial Reporting* (page **113**)
J The trial balance
   1 Uses and limitations of the trial balance
K Some concluding remarks
   1 The accounting cycle in perspective - see *A Second Look* (page **116**)

Topical coverage and suggested assignment

Class Meetings on Chapter	Topical Outline Coverage	Homework Assignment (To Be Completed Prior to Class)				
		Discussion Questions	Exercises	Problems	Cases	Internet
1	A - D	1, 5, 8, 9	1			
2	E - G	12, 13, 17, 18	2, 4, 7, 8,11	1, 2, 3	1, 3	1
3	H - K	20, 21	12	4, 5		

Comments and observations

Teaching objectives for Chapter 3

Our objectives in presenting this chapter are to:

1 Establish the usefulness of accounting records in organizations.

2 Explain and illustrate the purpose, unit of organization, and format of ledger accounts.

3 Relate the rules for debiting and crediting balance sheet accounts to the "side" of the balance sheet on which the account appears.

4 Explain the double-entry system of accounting.

5 Explain and illustrate the purpose, unit of organization, and format of a general journal.

6 Explain the flow of financial information from the journal into the ledger accounts.

7 Explain the nature of *net income*, and define the terms *revenue* and *expenses*.

8 Illustrate the recording of revenue and expense transactions. Explain the debit and credit rules for these transactions in the context of the effects upon owner's equity.

9 Explain the *realization* principle and the *matching* principle, providing common examples. Contrast *accrual accounting* with cash flows.

New features in Chapter 3

The majority of the material in this chapter is drawn from Chapters 2 and 3 of the prior edition. The material has been reorganized and several prior topics have been deleted to produce a complete overview of the accounting cycle with minimal emphasis on procedural and mechanical details. The overwhelming majority of the end-of-chapter material has been completely revised to be consistent with the new content of this chapter.

General comments

Overnight Auto Service is used as a continuing example in Chapters 2 through 4. At the outset in Chapter 3, the activities of the company are limited to balance sheet transactions. This allows us to illustrate the mechanics of double-entry accounting and to show how changes in assets, liabilities, and owners' equity are recorded in accounting records before discussing the more complicated concepts of revenue and expense. This approach also enables us to illustrate a very simple "accounting cycle" — the "flow" of information from the initial recording of transactions through the accounting records — without first having to cover adjusting entries and closing entries.

Among the important concepts introduced in Chapter 3 is **double-entry accounting.** Although double-entry accounting and the related rules of debit and credit may sound procedural to some, we view the double-entry system as a truly ingenious device. Johann Goethe, the renowned eighteenth-century German poet and novelist, described this system as "one of the finest discoveries of the human intellect." The great power of double-entry accounting is its ability to record the components of profit and loss, that is, revenue and expenses, simultaneously with the related changes in assets and liabilities. Thus, any accounting system that develops an income statement as well as a balance sheet uses the principles of double entry.

In the first class meeting on Chapter 3, we introduce students to the uses of accounting records in organizations. It is fairly obvious that accounting records will be used to record day-to-day transactions and serve as the basis for developing financial statements, tax returns, and other accounting reports. Less obvious to students are the other purposes of accounting records including internal control and performance evaluation. Discussion Question *1* can be used as the basis for class discussion of these uses of accounting information. We go on to introduce **ledger accounts** as a vehicle for illustrating double-entry accounting. We stress the relationship between the entry to record an **increase** in an account's balance and the **"side"** of the balance sheet upon which the account appears. This simple relationship is not only useful to students in learning the rules of debits and credits, but is the very device that makes the double-entry system work.

In the first class meeting, we go on to introduce the **general journal** and focus upon the "flow" of information through the accounting records and into the financial statements (balance sheet). We stress the point that the journal and ledger contain the same information, differing only as to the unit of organization. The journal is organized by **transaction,** whereas the same data in the ledger is organized by **financial statement item.** (Some care should be taken to dispel the common misconception that "double entry" means recording the transaction in both the journal and the ledger.)

Our next overall objective in Chapter 3 is to show how business profits are defined and measured in an accounting system. We emphasize the definitions of revenue and expenses, and the realization and matching principles. We find Exercise *7* useful in making the point that net income is a change in **owners' equity**, not a change in assets.

Careful attention should be given to both the realization principle and the matching principle. These principles represent the basic difference between accrual accounting and cash transactions. Also, these principles underlie many of the concepts that will be discussed in later chapters. We introduce these principles during the first class meeting but discuss them again in the second class meeting, illustrating the application of these principles in realistic business situations. Cases *1* and *2* are intended for this purpose.

Supplemental Exercises

Business Week Exercise

Net income isn't all about the numbers. Social, political, and environmental issues can affect the income statement. See "Can Nike Still Do It?", *Business Week*, February 21, 2000. CEO Phil Knight is struggling to refuild the shoemaker from top to bottom after an outcry over working conditions in Nike's overseas factories started in the lates '90s.

Group Exercise

Chapter 3 begins with the assertion that a basic objective of every business is to earn a profit. Proof of this can usually be found in the self-stated missions and objectives of a business enterprise. For example, Procter and Gamble's 2001 Annual Report identified the following goal: "When we began the 2000/2001 fiscal yar, Job One was getting P % G's business back on track and growing again. We have refocused on our biggest, and fastest growing brands, in our biggest markets, with our leading customers. We've strengthened the value of our brands for consumers. We've made strategic choices about which businesses P&G should be in, and which it should not. And we've improved P&G's competitiveness by controlling costs and managing cash more effectively. We believe these are the choices that will deliver superior Total Shareholder Return, which is the key measure of our progress and our underlying commitment to P&G shareholders." Access the annual reports of other corporations and cite evidence that the pursuit of profit is a major objective. What other objectives or goals do these companies set forth?

Internet Exercise

In Chapter 3 we have learned that net income is an increase in owners' equity resulting from profitable operations. Previously, Chapter 2 explained that when a business is organized as a corporation, retained earnings represents the increase in stockholders' equity that has accumulated over the years as a result of profitable operations. Thus, net income for any one year should explain a large part of the change in retained earnings from the beginning of the year to the end. Of course, a net loss should explain a large part of the decrease in retained earnings from the beginning of the year to the end. Visit JC Penney's website at http://www.jcpenney.net/company/finance/archives/annual/2000/web14-17.pdf.

Find net loss for 2000. Now compute the difference between retained (reinvested) earnings at the beginning of the year and at the end. How closely does this approximate the 2000 net loss?

Indicate the best answer for each question in the space provided.

The account balances for HydroTech as of May 31, 2003, are listed below in alphabetical order:

Accounts Payable	$10,000	Equipment	$16,000
Accounts Receivable	12,000	Land	50,000
Building	40,000	Notes Payable	28,000
Capital Stock	76,000	Retained Earnings	10,000
Cash	6,000		

_____　**1**　***Refer to the above data.*** In a trial balance prepared on May 31, 2003, the sum of the ***debit column*** is:

　　　　　a　$124,000.　　　　　　　**c**　$144,000.
　　　　　b　$86,000.　　　　　　　　**d**　Some other amount.

On June 3, HydroTech collected $7,000 of its accounts receivable and paid $4,000 of its accounts payable. In addition, 480 additional shares of capital stock were issued for $2,400 cash.

_____　**2**　***Refer to the above data.*** On June 4, the balance in the ***Cash*** account is:

　　　　　a　$9,000.　　　　　　　　**c**　$11,400.
　　　　　b　$5,400.　　　　　　　　**d**　Some other amount.

_____　**3**　***Refer to the above data.*** On June 4, the balance in the ***Capital Stock*** account is:

　　　　　a　$88,400.　　　　　　　**c**　$76,000.
　　　　　b　$78,400.　　　　　　　**d**　Some other amount.

_____　**4**　***Refer to the above data.*** In a trial balance prepared on June 4, the sum of the ***credit column*** is:

　　　　　a　$113,000.　　　　　　　**c**　$115,400
　　　　　b　$122,400.　　　　　　　**d**　Some other amount.

_____　**5**　***Refer to the above data.*** On June 6, the bookkeeper for HydroTech makes this entry:

　　　　　Equipment... 6,300
　　　　　　　Cash.. 　　　　1,500
　　　　　　　Accounts Payable .... 　　　　4,800

This transaction:
a　Decreases total assets.
b　Involves the sale of equipment for $6,300.
c　Increases total assets $6,300.
d　Increases liabilities.

10 MINUTE QUIZ

CHAPTER 3   NAME_____ #_____

10-MINUTE QUIZ B   SECTION_____

Enter the following transactions in the two-column journal provided for Marc's Detailing. You may omit explanations.

Mar. 2   Purchased auto cleaning supplies from Pip Boys for $240 on account.
 4   Collected an account receivable of $470 from a customer, At-Your-Service Limousines.
 5   Paid $320 in partial payment of an account payable to Sears for equipment purchased in February.
 7   Issued capital stock in exchange for $2,500 cash.
 9   Purchased office quipment from Jerome's Warehouse for $3,300; paid $1,000 cash and issued a note payable due in 90 days for the balance.

Date	General Journal		
20__			
Mar 2			
4			
5			
7			
9			

CHAPTER 3   NAME_____ #_____

10-MINUTE QUIZ C   SECTION_____

Fagan Financial Advisors, Inc. had the following transactions during January, its first month or operations:

a.   Issued to Joan Fagan 8,000 shares of capital stock in exchange for her investment of $40,000 cash.
b.   Borrowed $20,000 from a bank and signed a note payable due in three months.
c.   Purchased office furniture costing $17,500; and paid $3,500 cash and charged the balance on account.
d.   Paid $7,000 of the amount owed for office furniture.
e.   Issued an additional 1,000 shares of capital stock to an individual who invests $5,000 in the business.

Instructions
Record the above transactions directly in the T accounts below. Identify each entry in a T account with the letter shown for the transaction.

Cash		Office Furnishings		Notes Payable

Accounts Payable		Capital Stock

The following transactions occurred during June, the first month of operations for Tower Engineering, Inc:

- Issued 80,000 shares of capital stock to the owners of the corporation in exchange for $800,000 cash.
- Purchased a piece of land for $400,000, making a $120,000 cash down payment and signing a note payable for the balance.
- Made a $100,000 cash payment on the note payable from the purchase of land.
- Purchased equipment on credit from CADPro for $56,000.

_____   1   *Refer to the above data.* What is the balance in the Cash account at the end of June?
              a $524,000.   c $580,000.
              b $344,000.   d $244,000.

_____   2   *Refer to the above data.* What are total assets of Tower Engineering at the end of June?
              a $800,000.   c $228,000.
              b $1,036,000.   d $290,000.

_____   3   *Refer to the above data.* What is the total of Tower's liabilities at the end of June?
              a $90,000.   c $336,000.
              b $1,036,000.   d $236,000.

_____   4   *Refer to the above data.* What is the total owners' equity at the end of June?
              a $800,000.   c $580,000.
              b $1,036,000.   d $524,000.

SOLUTIONS TO CHAPTER 3 10-MINUTE QUIZZES

QUIZ A
1 A
2 C
3 B
4 B
5 D

QUIZ B

Date	General Journal		
2001			
Mar 2	Supplies	240	
	Accounts Payable		240
	Bought supplies from Pip Boys.*		
4	Cash	470	
	Accounts Receivable		470
	Collected from At-Your-Service Limousines.*		
5	Accounts Payable	320	
	Cash		320
	Partial payment on amount due to Sears.*		
7	Cash	2,500	
	Capital Stock		2,500
	Issued capital stock.*		
9	Office Equipment	3,300	
	Cash		1,000
	Notes Payable		2,300
	Purchased office equipment from Jerome's		
	Warehouse; note due in 90 days.*		

*Note to instructor: Explanations not required in this quiz.

QUIZ C

Cash			Office Furnishings	
a. 40,000		c. 3,500	c. 17,500	
b. 20,000		d. 7,000		
e. 5,000				

Notes Payable		Accounts Payable	
	b. 20,000	d. 7,000	c. 14,000

Capital Stock	
	a. 40,000
	e. 5,000

QUIZ D

1 C
2 B
3 D
4 A

Assignment Guide to Chapter 3

	Exercises	Problems					Cases			Net
	1 - 13	1	2	3	4	5	1	2	3	1
Time estimate (in minutes)	<15	30	30	35	50	60	15	30	30	10
Difficulty rating	E	M	M	M	S	S	M	S	M	E
Learning Objectives:										
1. Identify the steps in the accounting cycle and discuss the role of accounting records in an organization.										
2. Describe a ledger account and a ledger.	1, 2, 5, 8, 9, 13				√	√				
3. State the rules of debit and credit for balance sheet accounts.	1, 4, 5, 8, 9, 13	√	√	√	√	√				
4. Explain the double-entry system of accounting.	1, 4, 5, 8, 9, 12	√	√	√	√	√				
5. Explain the purpose of a journal and its relationship to the ledger.	1, 2, 4, 5, 8, 9	√	√	√	√	√				
6. Explain the nature of net income, revenue, and expenses.	1, 3, 7, 8, 9, 10, 11, 12		√	√	√	√				√
7. Apply the realization and matching principles in recording revenue and expenses.	1, 3, 10, 11, 12, 13	√	√	√	√	√		√	√	
8. Explain why revenues are recorded with credits and expenses are recorded with debits.	1, 7, 12		√	√	√	√	√	√		
9. Prepare a trial balance and explain its uses and limitations.	1, 2, 6				√	√	√	√		
10. Distinguish between the accounting cycle procedures and the knowledge of accounting.	1, 2, 13	√			√	√	√	√		

THE ACCOUNTING CYCLE: ACCRUALS AND DEFERRALS

Chapter Summary

In order for revenues and expenses to be reported in which they are earned or incurred, adjusting entries must be made at the end of the accounting period. Adjusting entries are made so the revenue recognition and matching principles are followed. Chapter 4 completes the treatment of the accounting cycle for service type businesses. It focuses on the year-end activities culminating in the annual report. These include the preparation of adjusting entries, preparing the financial statements themselves, drafting the footnotes to the statements, closing the accounts, and preparing for the audit. These topics form the content of Chapter 4.

The chapter begins with a thorough review of various adjusting entries. The adjustments are classified into four categories: converting assets to expenses; converting liabilities to revenue; accruing unpaid expenses and; accruing uncollected revenues. The categories are discussed and illustrated in this order. We briefly explain that the adjusting entries are needed to satisfy the realization and matching principles. The concept of materiality is introduced and its relevance to the adjusting entries is explained next.

Learning Objectives

1. Explain the purpose of adjusting entries.

2. Describe and prepare the four basic types of adjusting entries.

3. Prepare adjusting entries to convert assets to expenses.

4. Prepare adjusting entries to convert liabilities to revenue.

5. Prepare adjusting entries to accrue unpaid expenses.

6. Prepare adjusting entries to accrue uncollected revenue.

7. Explain how the principles of realization and matching relate to adjusting entries.

8. Explain the concept of materiality.

9. Prepare an adjusted trial balance and describe its purpose.

Brief topical outline

    A   Adjusting entries
- **1**   The need for adjusting entries
- **2**   Types of adjusting entries - see Cash Effects (page **137**)
- **3**   Characteristics of adjusting entries
- **4**   Converting assets to expenses
  - **a** Prepaid expenses - see Management Strategy & Financial Reporting (page **140**)
  - **b** Shop supplies
  - **c** Insurance policies - see *Your Turn* (page **142**)
  - **d** Recording prepayments directly in the expense accounts
- **5**   The concept of depreciation
  - **a** What is deprecation?
  - **b** Depreciation is only an estimate - see *Case in Point* (page **143**)
  - **c** Depreciation of building
  - **d** Depreciation of tools and equipment - see *Cash Effects* (page **145**)
- **6**   Converting liabilities to revenue - see *Case in Point* (page **145**)
  - **a** Recording advance collections directly in the revenue accounts
- **7**   Accruing unpaid expenses
  - **a** Accrual of wages (or salaries) expense
  - **b** Accrual of interest expense
- **8**   Accruing uncollected revenue - see *Your Turn* (page **149**)
- **9**   Accruing income taxes expense: the final adjusting entry - see *Case in Point* (page **150**)
  - **a** Income taxes in unprofitable periods

    B   Adjusting entries and accounting principles - see *Your Turn* (page **152**)
- **1**   The concept of materiality
  - **a** Materiality and adjusting entries
  - **b** Materiality is a matter of professional judgment
- **2**   Effects of the adjusting entries

    C   Concluding remarks - see *A Second Look* (page **156**)

Topical coverage and suggested assignment

Class Meetings on Chapter	Topical Outline Coverage	Homework Assignment (To Be Completed Prior to Class)				
		Discussion Questions	Exercises	Problems	Cases	Internet
1	A	1, 2, 4	2, 3, 6	1		
2	A	8, 9	7, 9	3, 4	1	1
3	B - C	10, 11	10, 11	6	2	

Comments and observations

Teaching objectives for Chapter 4

In Chapter 4 we cover the numerous accounting activities, both analytical and procedural, that take place at the end of a fiscal year. In covering this chapter, our teaching objectives are to:

1   Explain the need for adjusting entries in accrual accounting.

2   Illustrate the four basic types of adjusting entries.

3   Review in sequence the steps in the complete accounting cycle.

4   Introduce the principle of *materiality* and discuss its relevance to adjusting entries.

New features in Chapter 4

Chapter 4 now contains our entire treatment of adjusting entries and an adjusted trial balance. Most of the end-of chapter material has been rewritten to accommodate this change in organization.

General comments

The need for adjusting entries stems from the most basic concepts of accrual accounting, the concepts that revenue is recognized when it is *earned* and that expenses are recognized when the related goods and services are used. We find that students who do not fully understand the nature and purpose of adjusting entries have difficulty with other accrual accounting concepts throughout the course. We find Exercises *2, 3, 5,* and *9* particularly useful. Exercise *2* illustrates the effects of the four basic types of adjusting entries upon both the income statement and balance sheet. Exercise *3* focuses upon those adjustments that apportion previously recorded amounts, while Exercise *5* illustrates adjustments needed to accrue unrecorded amounts. Exercise *9* demonstrates that the need for adjusting entries arises from transactions spanning more than one accounting period. We also like Exercise *6,* which focuses upon unearned revenue in the accounting records of *American Airlines.*

We personally spend quite a bit of class time on *materiality,* as we consider it to be one of the most important concepts in accounting. The chapter has several good assignments on materiality, including Discussion Questions *10* and *11,* Exercise *10,* and Case *2.* We always assign at least two of these and discuss them in class.

An aside   Some students may ask why the word "debit" is abbreviated "Dr." in the columnar headings of the worksheet, as there is no "r" in "debit." The word "debit" is derived from the Latin verb *debere,* which means "to owe." "Credit" stems from the Latin verb *credere,* meaning "to entrust" or "to lend." In modern usage, of course, the term *debit* has come to mean any entry in the left-hand side of a ledger account, and *credit* has come to mean any entry in the right-hand side.

Supplemental Exercises

Business Week Exercise

Review the antitrust suit brought against Microsoft in "Bill Gates Isn't in the Clear Yet", *Business Week*, March 18, 2002. As a stockholder would you regard this information about the company as relevant? How would Microsoft have communicated this information to external parties?

Group Exercise

Have students interview accounting managers at several corporations in the local area. Ask students to find out how often the corporation prepares adjusting entries and how important the accounting manager thinks adjusting entries are to the fair presentation of the financial statements to the stockholders and creditors.

Internet Exercise

Visit the homepage of Microsoft at www.microsoft.com. Access the annual report for 2001. Find the footnotes to the statements and read the disclosures in the note titled "Contingencies." Regarding the events described do you think Microsoft is providing adequate disclosure to its stockholders?

Indicate the best answer for each question in the space provided.

_____ 1   Hampton Jewelers purchased display shelves on March 1 for $9,000. If this asset has an estimated useful life of five years, what is the *book value* of the display shelves on April 30?
  a $150.   b $8,700.   c $8,850.   d $300.

_____ 2   The adjusting entry to recognize an unrecorded expense is necessary:
  a   When an expense is paid in advance.
  b   When an expense has been neither paid nor recorded as of the end of the accounting period.
  c   Whenever an expense remains unpaid at the end of an accounting period.
  d   Because the accountant is likely to forget to pay these unrecorded expenses.

_____ 3   Before any month-end adjustments are made, the next income of Gannett Company is $80,000. However, the following adjustments are necessary: office supplies used, $1,500; services performed for clients but not yet recorded or collected, $25,00; interest accrued on note payable to bank,$4,500. After adjusting entries are made for the items listed above, Gannett Company's net income would be:
  a $76,500.   b $82,300.   c $81,500.   d $82,700.

_____ 4   Of the following adjusting entries, which one results in an increase in liabilities and the recognition of an expense at the end of an accounting period?
  a   The entry to accrue salaries owed to employees at the end of the period.
  b   The entry to record revenue earned but not yet collected or recorded.
  c   The entry to record earned portion of rent previously received in advance from a tenant.
  d   The entry to write off a portion of unexpired insurance.

_____ 5   The CPA firm auditing Greer Company found that net income had been overstated. Which of the following errors could be the cause?
  a   Failure to record depreciation expense for the period.
  b   No entry made to record purchase of land for cash on the last day of the year.
  c   Failure to record payment of an account payable on the last day of the year.
  d   Failure to make an adjusting entry to record revenue that had been earned but not yet billed to customers.

CHAPTER 4   NAME_____ #_____

10-MINUTE QUIZ B   SECTION_____

Wet World Water Park adjusts its books each month and closes its books on December 31 each year. The trial balance at January 31, 2001, *before* adjustments, follows:

	Debit	Credit
Cash	$ 6,600	
Supplies	5,400	
Unexpired Insurance	12,600	
Equipment	72,000	
Accumulated Depreciation: Equipment		$ 18,000
Unearned Admission Revenue		12,000
Capital Stock		20,000
Retained Earnings, January 1, 2001		38,200
Admissions Revenue		27,600
Salaries Expense	8,100	
Utilities Expense	5,700	
Rent Expense	5,400	
	$115,800	$115,800

_____ 1 *Refer to the above data.* According to attendance records, $7,800 of the Unearned Admission Revenue has been earned in January. Compute the amount of admissions revenue to be shown in the January *income statement*:
   a $35,400.   **b** $19,800.   **c** $7,800.   **d** $4,200.

_____ 2 *Refer to the above data.* At January 31, the amount of supplies on hand is $1,050. What amount is shown on the January income statement for *supplies expense*?
   a $1,050.   **b** $5,400.   **c** $6,450.   **d** $4,350.

_____ 3 *Refer to the above data.* The equipment has an original estimated useful life of eight years. Compute the *book value* of the equipment at January 31 after the proper January adjustment is recorded:
   a $750.   **b** $72,000.   **c** $53,250.   **d** $49,500.

_____ 4 *Refer to the above data.* Employees are owed $1,200 for services since the last payday in January to be paid the first week of February. No adjustment was made for this item. As a result of this error:
   a Assets at January 31 are overstated.
   b January net income is overstated.
   c Liabilities at January 31 are overstated.
   d Owner's equity at January 31 is understated.

_____   **5**   ***Refer to the above data.*** On August 1, 2000, the park purchased a 12-month insurance policy. The necessary adjusting entry at January 31 includes which of the following entries? (Hint: The company has adjusted its books ***monthly***.)

a   A debit to Insurance Expense for $1,050.

b   A credit to Unexpired Insurance for $11,550.

c   A credit to Unexpired Insurance for $1,800.

d   A debit to Unexpired Insurance for $10,800.

Wet World Water Park adjusts its books each month and closes its books on December 31 each year. The trial balance at January 31, 2001, *before* adjustments, follows:

	Debit	Credit
Cash	$ 4,400	
Supplies	3,600	
Unexpired Insurance	8,400	
Equipment	48,000	
Accumulated Depreciation: Equipment		$12,000
Unearned Admission Revenue		8,000
Capital Stock		10,000
Retained Earnings, January 1, 2001		28,800
Admissions Revenue		18,400
Salaries Expense	5,400	
Utilities Expense	3,800	
Rent Expense	3,600	
	$77,200	$77,200

1 *Refer to the above data.* According to attendance records, $5,200 of the Unearned Admission Revenue has been earned in January. Compute the balance in the following accounts after the proper adjustment is made.
   Unearned Admission Revenue account balance $_____
   Admission Revenue account balance $_____

2 *Refer to the above data.* At January 31, the amount of supplies still on hand was determined to be $700.   What amount should be reported in the January income statement for *supplies expense*? $_____

3 *Refer to the above data.* The equipment has an original useful life of eight years. Compute the *book value* of the equipment at January 31 *after* the proper January adjustment is recorded.
                                                                                 $_____

4 *Refer to the above data.* $800 is owed to employees for work since the last payday in January, to be paid the first week of February. What is the effect on *January net income* if the accountant fails to make any January 31 adjustment for this item? January net income will be (overstated/understated) by $_____.

5 *Refer to the above data.* On June 1, 2000, the park purchased a 12-month insurance policy. Give the adjusting entry to record insurance coverage expiring in January. (Hint: The company adjusts its books *monthly*.)

CHAPTER 4   NAME_____ #_____

10-MINUTE QUIZ D   SECTION_____

The accountant for Timesure Inc. prepared the following trial balance at January 31, 2000, after *one month* of operations:

	Debit	Credit
Cash	$ 5,400	
Accounts Receivable	4,200	
Unexpired Insurance	1,800	
Office Equipment	18,000	
Unearned Consulting Fees		$ 3,000
Capital Stock		15,300
Retained Earnings, January 1, 2000		0
Dividends	3,000	
Consulting Fees Earned		25,000
Salaries Expense	7,400	
Utilities Expense	1,400	
Rent Expense	1,800	
Supplies	300	
	$43,300	$43,300

Additional information:

a   Consulting services rendered to a client in January, not yet billed or recorded, $1,900.

b   Portion of insurance expiring in January, $150.

c   Income taxes expense for January of $2,000.

d   The office equipment has a life of 5 years.

Instructions: Prepare adjusting entries for a through d.

	Adjusting Entries		
Jan. 31			

SOLUTIONS TO CHAPTER 4   10-MINUTE QUIZZES

QUIZ A
1   B
2   B
3   A
4   A
5   A

QUIZ B
1   A
2   D
3   C
4   B
5   C

QUIZ C

1
Unearned Admission Revenue: $8,000 − $5,200 = $2,800 credit
Admission Revenue: $18,400 + $5,200 = $23,600 credit

2
$3,600 - $700 = $2,900

3
January depreciation = $48,000 ÷ 8 × (1/12) = $500
$48,000 - $12,000 - $500 = $35,500 book value

4
Net income is overstated by $800.

5

Insurance Expense	1,680	
Unexpired Insurance...		1,680

Computation $8,400 ÷ 5 months remaining = $1,680 per month

QUIZ D

		Adjusting Entries		
Jan. 31	Accounts receivable		1,900	
	Consulting fees earned			1,900
31	Insurance expense		150	
	Unexpired insurance			150
31	Income tax expense		2,000	
	Income tax payable			2,000
31	Depreciation expense		300	
	Accumulated depreciation			300

Assignment Guide to Chapter 4

	Exercises	Problems						Cases			Net
	1 - 11	1	2	3	4	5	6	1	2	3	1
Time estimate (in minutes)	<15	40	40	25	30	60	25	30	30	30	25
Difficulty rating	E	M	M	S	M	S	E	M	M	M	M
Learning Objectives:											
1. Explain the purpose of adjusting entries.	1, 2, 3, 4, 5, 6, 7, 8, 9, 11, 12	√	√	√	√	√	√	√			√
2. Describe and prepare the four basic types of adjusting entries.	1, 2, 3, 4, 5, 6, 7, 8, 9, 11, 12	√	√	√	√	√	√	√			√
3. Prepare adjusting entries to convert assets to expenses.	1, 2, 3, 4, 5, 7, 9, 11	√	√	√	√	√	√	√			√
4. Prepare adjusting entries to convert liabilities to revenue.	1, 2, 3, 4, 5, 6, 7, 9, 11	√	√	√	√	√	√	√		√	√
5. Prepare adjusting entries to accrue unpaid expenses.	1, 2, 3, 4, 5, 7, 8, 9, 11	√	√	√	√	√	√	√			√
6. Prepare adjusting entries to accrue uncollected revenue.	1, 2, 3, 4, 5, 7, 9, 11	√	√	√	√	√	√	√		√	√
7. Explain how the principles of *realization* and *matching* related to adjusting entries.	1, 3, 4, 5, 9, 11	√	√	√	√	√	√	√	√		
8. Explain the concept of *materiality*.	1, 10, 11								√		
9. Prepare an adjusted trial balance and describe its purpose.	1, 2, 7, 9		√	√	√	√	√				

©The McGraw-Hill Companies, Inc., 2003
Instructor's Resource Manual

Chapter Summary

Chapter 5 completes the treatment of the accounting cycle for service type businesses. It focuses on the year-end activities culminating in the annual report. These include the preparation of the financial statements, adequate disclosure, closing the accounts, and preparing for the audit. These topics form the content of Chapter 5.

The preparation of the statements from an adjusted trial balance is explained and illustrated. Added to this coverage are a discussion of adequate disclosure and the preparation of footnotes to the statements. The closing process is described in detail and illustrated for the Overnight Auto Service Case. Overnight's financial results are analyzed briefly in terms of profitability and solvency.

The chapter ends with a discussion of how interim financial statements are prepared by a business that closes its accounts only at year-end.

Our *Supplemental Topic* on the worksheet is repeated from the prior edition. We approach the worksheet as a pedagogical tool intended to provide the student with a better grasp of the year-end procedures.

Learning Objectives

1. Prepare an income statement, a statement of retained earnings, and a balance sheet.

2. Explain how the income statement and the statement of retained earnings relate to the balance sheet.

3. Explain the concept of *adequate disclosure.*

4. Explain the purpose of *closing entries*; prepare these entries.

5. Prepare an after-closing trial balance.

6. Use financial statement information to evaluate profitability and solvency.

7. Explain how *interim* financial statements are prepared in a business that closes its accounts only at year-end.

*8. Prepare a worksheet and explain its usefulness.

*Supplemental Topic, "The Worksheet."

Brief topical outline

A   Preparing financial statements - see *Case in Point* (page **176**)
     1   The income statement
     2   The statement of retained earnings
        a   A word about dividends
     3   The balance sheet
B   Relationship among the financial statements
     1   Drafting the notes that accompany financial statements - see *Cash Effects* (page **181**)
     2   What types of information must be disclosed? - see *Your Turn* (page **182**)
C   Closing the temporary equity accounts
     1   Closing entries for revenue accounts
     2   Closing entries for expense accounts
     3   Closing the income summary account
     4   Closing the dividends account - see *Your Turn* (page **187**)
D   Summary of the closing entries
E   After-closing trial balance
     1   Evaluating profitability - see *Management Strategy* (page **189**)
     2   Evaluating liquidity - see *Cash Effects* (page **189**)
F   Financial analysis
     1   Preparing financial statements covering different periods of time
G   Concluding remarks - see *A Second Look* (page **192**)
Supplemental Topic
* H   The worksheet
     1   Isn't this really a "spreadsheet"?
     2   How is a worksheet used?
     3   The mechanics: how its done
        a   Computers do the pencil-pushing
     4   What-if: a special application of worksheet software

Topical coverage and suggested assignment

Class Meetings on Chapter	Topical Outline Coverage	Homework Assignment (To Be Completed Prior to Class)				
		Discussion Questions	Exercises	Problems	Cases	Internet
1	A - C	2, 5, 6	2, 3	1	2,3	1
2	D - F	7, 8, 9, 16	4, 7, 9, 10	2, 3, 5, 8		2
3	G - *H	*17		4, 6		

*Optional assignment, time permitting.

Comments and observations

Teaching objectives for Chapter 5

In Chapter 5 we cover the numerous accounting activities, both analytical and procedural, that take place at the end of a fiscal year. The worksheet is discussed in a **Supplemental Topic** section which we view as optional. In covering this chapter, our teaching objectives are to:

1   Show how the financial statements may be prepared from the adjusted trial balance.

2   Explain relationships among the financial statements.

3   Discuss drafting of the notes that accompany the financial statements.

4   Present closing entries and an after-closing trial balance.

*5   Explain and illustrate the use of a worksheet *(optional topic)*.

New features in Chapter 5

Our coverage of the closing process, adjusted trial balance, statement preparation, and the after-closing trial balance are all placed in Chapter 5.

General comments

We consider our emphasis on **adequate disclosure** and the preparation of **footnotes** a significant feature of Chapter 5. This material is clearly important to the user of financial statements, and should be given sufficient time for class discussion. We find Case *2* well suited to this purpose.

   We then spend quite a bit of class time on closing entries and preparing an after-closing trial balance. The chapter has several good assignments on closing entries, including Discussion Questions *9* and *10*, Exercise *5*, and Problem *2*. We always assign at least two of these and discuss them in class.

   How much time, if any, should you spend covering the worksheet? There is no question that the importance of a worksheet in actual accounting practice has declined significantly. Most computer-based systems do not print out a 10-column worksheet. Rather, they print the various elements of the worksheet--trial balances, adjusting entries, and financial statements--as a series of separate schedules. In manual accounting systems, many accountants carry the worksheet only through the adjusted trial balance columns and then prepare formal financial statements. Thus, one might argue that today's students are not likely to see a 10-column worksheet outside of their accounting class.

Still, we find the worksheet to be a valuable pedagogical tool, and have therefore retained it in this edition as a *Supplemental Topic*. Preparing a worksheet gives students a better understanding of the end-of-period adjusting and closing procedures. It helps them to see the relationships between the trial balance and financial statements, as well as the relationship between the income statement and the balance sheet. In short, we now view a 10-column worksheet as a teaching device: a *flowchart with numbers*, rather than a schedule that students should learn to prepare. Thorough coverage can be achieved by assigning Problem *7*.

Supplemental Exercise

Business Week Exercise

Changes are taking place in Japan's economic system that promise to benefit both Japan and its global partners. As companies and financial institutions begin to modernize, structural barriers to trade are beginning to fall. Review "Don't Look Now, But a New Japan is Taking Shape", *Business Week*, May 29, 2000. What are some methods Japan is using to eliminate excess capacity and improve *profitability*?

Group Exercise

This exercise modifies Case 5-1. Have the groups follow the same instructions given in the case but now use the question: *Is it ethical for a CPA (or a CPA firm) to provide both consulting services and audits to the same companies?*

Internet Exercise

Visit the homepage of Ford at www.ford.com. Access the annual report for 2001. Find the footnotes to the statements and read the disclosures in the note titled "Contingencies." Regarding the events described, do you think Ford is providing adequate disclosure to its stockholders?

The accountant for Gwiz Consulting prepared the following "adjusted" trial balance at December 31, 2000, after one year of operations:

	Debit	Credit
Cash	$ 5,400	
Accounts Receivable	4,200	
Unexpired Insurance	1,800	
Office Equipment	18,000	
Accumulated Depreciation: Office Equipment		$ 300
Unearned Consulting Fees		3,000
Capital Stock		15,000
Retained Earnings, January 1, 2000		0
Dividends	3,000	
Consulting Fees Earned		25,000
Salaries Expense	7,400	
Utilities Expense	1,400	
Rent Expense	1,800	
Depreciation Expense	300	
	$43,300	$43,300

Prepare the closing entries for Gwiz Consulting.

	Closing Entries		
Dec. 31			

10 MINUTE QUIZ

CHAPTER 5   NAME_____ #_____

10-MINUTE QUIZ B   SECTION_____

Presented below is the adjusted trial balance of TWK, Inc. at December 31:

	Debit	Credit
Cash	$ 10	
Accounts Receivable	20	
Equipment	200	
Accounts Payable		$ 15
Capital Stock		100
Retained Earnings		50
Dividends	5	
Service Revenue		180
Salaries Expense	80	
Depreciation Expense	20	
Supplies Expense	10	
	$345	$345

_____ 1 ***Refer to the above data.*** What is the balance in income summary before it is closed to retained earnings?

   a $65.   b $70.   c $75.   d $180.

_____ 2 ***Refer to the above data.*** What is the balance in retained earnings at December 31?

   a $70.   b $115.   c $65.   d $50.

_____ 3 ***Refer to the above data.*** What are the total debits on the after-closing trial balance?

   a $345.   b $395.   c $280.   d $415.

_____ 4 ***Refer to the above data.*** Which accounts are closed to income summary?

   a All accounts.
   b Revenues and expenses.
   c Revenues, expenses, and dividends.
   d All accounts that are not nominal.

_____ 5 ***Refer to the above data.*** Which accounts will appear on the balance sheet?

   a Retained earnings of $50.
   b Dividends of $5.
   c Net income of $65.
   d None of the above.

©The McGraw-Hill Companies, Inc., 2003
Instructor's Resource Manual

CHAPTER 5   NAME_____ #_____

10-MINUTE QUIZ C   SECTION_____

The accountant for Gwiz Consulting prepared the following "adjusted" trial balance at December 31, 2002, after one year of operations:

	Debit	Credit
Cash	$ 5,400	
Accounts Receivable	4,200	
Unexpired Insurance	1,800	
Office Equipment	18,000	
Accumulated Depreciation: Office Equipment		$ 300
Unearned Consulting Fees		3,000
Capital Stock		15,000
Retained Earnings, January 1, 2000		0
Dividends	3,000	
Consulting Fees Earned		25,000
Salaries Expense	7,400	
Utilities Expense	1,400	
Rent Expense	1,800	
Depreciation Expense	300	
	$43,300	$43,300

Prepare an after-closing Trial Balance.

CHAPTER 5   NAME_____ #_____

10-MINUTE QUIZ D   SECTION_____

Dinos, Inc.
Trial Balance
December 31

	Debit	Credit
Cash	$ 12	
Accounts Receivable	30	
Equipment	170	
Accounts Payable		$ 18
Capital Stock		100
Retained Earnings		30
Dividends	4	
Service Revenue		183
Salaries Expense	90	
Depreciation Expense	18	
Advertising Expense	7	
	$331	$331

Prepare the closing entries.

	Closing Entries		
Dec. 31			

SOLUTIONS TO CHAPTER 5   10-MINUTE QUIZZES

QUIZ A

Closing Entries

		Debit	Credit
Dec. 31	Retained Earnings	3,000	
	Dividends		3,000
31	Consulting Fees Earned	25,000	
	Income Summary		25,000
31	Income Summary	10,900	
	Salaries Expense		7,400
	Utilities Expense		1,400
	Rent Expense		1,800
	Depreciation Expense		300
31	Retained Earnings	14,100	
	Income Summary		14,100

QUIZ B

1 B
2 B
3 C
4 B
5 D

QUIZ C

	Debit	Credit
Cash	$ 5,400	
Accounts Receivable	4,200	
Unexpired Insurance	1,800	
Office Equipment	18,000	
Accumulated Depreciation		$ 300
Unearned Consulting Fees		3,000
Capital Stock		15,000
Retained Earnings, Jan. 31, 2001		11,100
	$29,400	$29,400

QUIZ D

Closing Entries

Dec. 31	Retained Earnings		4	
	Dividends			4
31	Service Revenue		183	
	Income Summary			183
31	Income Summary		115	
	Salaries Expense			90
	Depreciation Expense			18
	Advertising Expense			7
31	Retained Earnings		68	
	Income Summary			68

Assignment Guide to Chapter 5

	Exercises	Problems								Cases			Net
	1-10	1	2	3	4	5	6	7	8	1	2	3	1
Time estimate (in minutes)	<15	40	40	25	30	60	50	50	30	30	30	30	25
Difficulty rating	E	M	M	S	M	S	S	S	M	M	M	M	M
Learning Objectives:													
1. Prepare an income statement, a statement of retained earnings, and a balance sheet.	1, 2, 3, 8									√			
2. Explain how the income statement and the statement of retained earnings relate to the balance sheet.	1, 2, 3, 4, 5, 6, 7, 8, 9		√	√	√	√						√	
3. Explain the concept of *adequate disclosure*.	1, 9, 10		√	√	√	√					√	√	√
4. Explain the purposes of *closing entries*; prepare these entries.	1, 4, 5, 6, 7	√	√	√	√	√							
5. Prepare an after-closing trial balance.	1, 4, 5	√	√	√									
6. Use financial statement information to evaluate profitability and solvency.	1, 2, 3, 10	√	√	√	√	√			√			√	
7. Explain how *interim* financial statements are prepared in a business that closes its accounts only at year-end.							√	√					
*8. Prepare a worksheet and explain its usefulness.	1, 8												

Chapter Summary

The introduction of merchandising provides a rich set of challenges for the student. These range from the problem of how to best account for the acquisition and sale of inventory to the development of accounting information to support the operating decisions of owners and managers.

The chapter opens with an introduction to the nature of a merchandising business. This discussion centers on the operating cycle of the merchandising business, and introduces the new concepts found on the income statement of a merchandiser. The nature and use of subsidiary ledgers is next introduced. Our intent is to demonstrate to the student that a single information system can be designed to serve multiple objectives. In this case, the accounting system provides the information required to meet financial reporting obligations, and through the use of subsidiary ledgers, produces the information required to serve the needs of company personnel in conducting daily business operations. Subsidiary ledgers for receivables, payables, and inventory are covered.

The core of the chapter explains the use of the perpetual and periodic inventory systems. Emphasis is placed on three topics: recording the acquisition of merchandise inventory, recording the sale of merchandise, and the determination of the cost of goods sold for presentation on the income statement. The relative merits of the two inventory systems are discussed in closing the section.

Numerous modifications to the accounting system designed to improve its efficiency are covered in some detail. We begin with a brief introduction to the nature of special journals. This is followed by an extensive discussion of additional transactions relating to purchases and sales. Topics covered include: recording purchases by the net and gross price methods, recording purchase returns, transportation costs, recording sales discounts and sales returns and allowances, delivery expenses, and accounting for sales taxes.

The chapter concludes by demonstrating the use of gross profit in evaluating the performance of a merchandising company.

Learning Objectives

1. Describe the ***operating cycle*** of a merchandising company.

2. Define ***subsidiary ledgers*** and explain their usefulness.

3. Account for purchases and sales of merchandise in a ***perpetual*** inventory system.

4. Explain how a ***periodic*** inventory system operates.

5. Discuss the factors to be considered in selecting an inventory system.

6. Define ***special journals*** and explain their usefulness.

7. Account for additional merchandising transactions related to purchases and sales.

8. Measure the performance of a merchandising business.

Brief topical outline

A Merchandising companies
   1 The operating cycle of a merchandising company
     a Comparing merchandising activities with manufacturing activities
     b Retailers and wholesalers – see *Case in Point* (page **223**)
   2 Income statement of a merchandising company
   3 What accounting information does a merchandising company need?
   4 General ledger accounts
   5 Subsidiary ledger accounts - see *Case in Point* (page **224**)
     a Subsidiary ledgers needed for merchandising transactions
     b Other types of subsidiary ledgers
     c Subsidiary ledgers in computer-based systems - see *Your Turn* (page **226**)
   6 Two approaches used in accounting for merchandising transactions
B Perpetual inventory systems
   1 Purchases of merchandise
   2 Sales of merchandise
   3 Payment of accounts payable to suppliers
   4 Collection of accounts receivable from customers
   5 The inventory subsidiary ledger
   6 Taking a physical inventory
   7 Closing entries in a perpetual inventory system - see *Your Turn* (page **230**)
C Periodic inventory systems
   1 Operation of a periodic inventory system
   2 Recording purchases of merchandise
   3 Computing cost of goods sold
   4 Recording inventory and cost of goods sold
   5 Closing process in a periodic inventory system
     a Creating cost of goods sold account
     b Completing the closing process
   6 Comparison of perpetual and periodic inventory systems
     a Who uses perpetual systems? - see *Case in Point* (page **234**)
     b Who uses periodic systems? - see *Case in Point* (page **235**)
   7 Selecting an inventory system
     a The trend in today's business world - see *Your Turn* (page **235**)

  D Modifying an accounting system
    1 Special journals provide speed and efficiency
  E Transactions relating to purchases
    1 Credit terms and cash discounts
      a Recording purchases at gross invoice price - see *Management Strategy* (page **238**)
    2 Returns of unsatisfactory merchandise
    3 Transportation costs on purchases
  F Transactions relating to sales
    1 Sales returns and allowances
    2 Sales discounts
    3 Delivery expenses
    4 Accounting for sales taxes
  G Evaluating the performance of a merchandising company
    1 Net sales
  H Financial analysis
    1 Gross profit margins
      a The overall gross profit margin
      b Departmental profit margins
      c Profit margins for individual products - see *Cash Effects* and *A Second Look* (page **244**)

Topical coverage and suggested assignment

Class Meetings on Chapter	Topical Outline Coverage	Homework Assignment (To Be Completed Prior to Class)				
		Discussion Questions	Exercises	Problems	Cases	Internet
1	A - B	1, 2, 3, 6	2, 3, 4	1, 2, 5		
2	C - D	10, 11	6, 7, 8, 13		1	1
3	E - H	13, 17, 18, 20	5, 9, 10, 11	4, 6	5	1

Comments and observations

Teaching objectives for Chapter 6

Our objectives in presenting this chapter are to:

1 Describe the operating cycle of a merchandising company.

2 Explain the role of subsidiary ledgers in an accounting system.

3 Account for purchases and sale of merchandise using a perpetual inventory system.

4 Describe accounting for purchases and sale of merchandise using a periodic inventory system.

5 Distinguish between perpetual and periodic inventory systems.

6 Illustrate accounting for cash discounts, merchandise returns, transportation costs, and sales taxes.

7 Demonstrate the computation and interpretation of gross profit margins.

New features in Chapter 6

Our coverage of accounting for merchandising activities is generally unchanged from the previous edition. Chapter 6 maintains our emphasis on perpetual inventory systems. The discussion of special journals is entirely descriptive and does not require the manipulation of any special journals. This section of the chapter also includes the material on purchase and sales discounts, returns and allowances, and sales taxes. A new exercise is based on analysis of Tootsie Roll's annual report included in Appendix A. Virtually all of the problem material has been rewritten for this edition.

General comments

We continue to use the perpetual inventory system as our primary means of accounting for inventories and the cost of goods sold. This reflects our goal of developing students' understanding of the real-world environment in which accounting information is developed and used. Today, all large businesses — and many small ones — use perpetual inventory systems. Because of the increasing use of inventory software by even the smallest business operations, the trend toward perpetual systems is certain to continue.

We also find that perpetual systems are considerably easier for students to understand. The periodic model — beginning inventory + purchases - ending inventory — is not a familiar concept to the introductory student. Also, this model seems to undermine the very concept of accounting providing useful (in this case, timely) information to decision makers. (We dislike being asked whether managers can run a business if accounting information is available only at annual intervals.) The evaluation of merchandising operations via gross profit rates emphasizes the timeliness of the information provided by a perpetual system. A perpetual system not only provides timely information but also follows the same "flow of costs" as has been described for office supplies, prepaid insurance, and depreciable assets. That is, when an asset is acquired, its cost is debited to an asset account; when the asset is consumed in business operations, its cost is transferred to an expense account.

In illustrating the flow of merchandise through a perpetual inventory system, we quickly review Exercise *4,* which takes only a couple of minutes, and reinforce the concepts with a thorough review of Problem *1.* We especially recommend Problem *1,* because it requires students to *interpret* and *use* the information that they have developed.

We use Exercise *13* to introduce the periodic system that illustrates not only the mechanics of this method but also the environment in which it is most likely to be found. We also recommend Case *1* for highlighting the environmental factors leading to a choice of inventory system. One of our Group Assignments, Case *4*, addresses the same issues and may be used to reinforce Case *1*.

We also stress the need for an annual physical inventory even when a perpetual system is in use, and review the adjusting entry to record shrinkage loss. Without this discussion, some students are confused by the fact that many businesses record sales transactions on modern point-of-sale terminals but then are still "Closed for Taking Inventory," or offer "Inventory Clearance Sales" near year-end.

The emphasis upon subsidiary ledgers Traditionally, subsidiary ledgers have been grouped with special journals and considered as procedural "bookkeeping" topics. We do not agree. Our new material on special journals makes the point that they are intended to improve the efficiency of the accounting system. Subsidiary ledgers, however, *provide information which is not available in the general ledger* but which is essential in *many daily business operations.* Anyone making use of accounting information within a particular business entity needs to know the types of information contained in the company's subsidiary ledgers. Both of our new Your Turn capsules included in this chapter reinforce the point. We highly recommend both of these discussion cases. To accomplish our objectives with respect to subsidiary ledgers, we refer the class to the illustrations on page **224**, and also instruct students to review Problem *2.*

Supplemental Exercises

Business Week Exercise

"NIKE'S Feet of Clay," *Business Week,* May 20, 2002, describes the company's problems with NIKE'S Air Jordan shoes. Inventory levels remain high. Various reasons are cited for the lack of sales including the shoe's high cost, $200 a pair. After reading the article, decide on some strategies NIKE could employ to boost the sales of its Air Jordans.

Group Exercise

The concept of internal control will be introduced in conjunction with Cash in Chapter 7. This chapter hints at one form of strong internal control in the form of the Purchases Discounts Lost account. For a merchandise company internal control over inventory is critical to success. Interview a local business and determine what internal controls are in place to: 1) safeguard its inventory assets and 2) assure that inventory is accounted for as accurately as possible.

If Case *6-4* was assigned, the same businesses could be used as the subjects for this study as well.

Internet Exercise

Revisit the homepages of MCI at www.mci.com and The Gap at www.gap.com. Select their most recent annual reports and compare the two companies in terms of the values of their inventories.

Indicate the best answer for each question in the space provided.

_____ 1   Which of the following businesses is most likely to use a periodic inventory system?
   a   An aircraft manufacturer.
   b   A supermarket which is part of a national chain.
   c   An independently owned art gallery with a manual accounting system.
   d   A beer bar.

_____ 2   A periodic inventory system eliminates the need for:
   a   Taking an annual physical inventory.
   b   Recording the revenue from sales transactions.
   c   Recording the cost of merchandise sold as sales occur.
   d   None of the above.

_____ 3   If management wants to know the cost and quantity of merchandise on hand at all times, the business will probably:
   a   Use a periodic inventory system.
   b   Maintain an inventory subsidiary ledger.
   c   Take a complete physical inventory each day.
   d   Debit all purchases of merchandise directly to the Cost of Goods Sold account.

_____ 4   In a perpetual inventory system, the entry to record the cost of goods sold always includes an entry of equal amount to the:
   a   Inventory account.
   b   Sales account.
   c   Purchases account.
   d   None of the above.

_____ 5   Prior to taking a physical inventory at year-end, the perpetual inventory records of Gifts'n Such showed an inventory of $25,000, sales of $350,000, and a cost of goods sold of $200,000. The year-end physical inventory indicated merchandise on hand costing $23,000. The company's gross profit for the year was:
   a $348,000.
   b $152,000.
   c $148,000.
   d   Some other amount.

10 MINUTE QUIZ

CHAPTER 6 NAME_____ #_____

10-MINUTE QUIZ B SECTION_____

At the end of last year, Appler, Inc. had merchandise costing $120,000 in inventory. During January of the current year, the company purchased merchandise costing $70,000, and sold merchandise that it had purchased at a total cost of $50,000.

Based upon the above information, place the best answer in the space provided. In questions 1 through 3, assume that Appler uses a *perpetual* inventory system.

_____ 1 The total *debited to the Inventory account* during January was:
       a $0.   c $70,000.
       b $50,000.   d Some other answer.

_____ 2 The *balance* in the Inventory account at January 31 was:
       a $50,000.   c $140,000.
       b $240,000.   d Some other answer.

_____ 3 The amount of costs transferred from the Inventory account to the Cost of Goods Sold account during January was:
       a $0.   c $70,000.
       b $50,000.   d Some other answer.

In questions 4 through 6, assume that Appler, Inc. uses a *periodic* inventory system and takes a physical inventory *only at year-end*.

_____ 4 The total *debited to the Inventory account* during January was:
       a $0.   c $70,000.
       b $50,000.   d Some other answer.

_____ 5 The *balance* in the Inventory account at January 31 was:
       a $0.   c $120,000.
       b $140,000.   d Some other answer.

_____ 6 The amount of costs transferred from the Inventory account to the Cost of Goods Sold account during January was:
       a $0.   c $70,000.
       b $50,000.   d Some other answer.

At the end of last year, Sports Center had merchandise costing $210,000 in inventory. During January of the current year, the company purchased merchandise costing $93,000, and sold merchandise that it had purchased at a total cost of $81,000.

a   Assume that Sports Center uses a *perpetual* inventory system.
      (1) The total amount debited to the Inventory account during January was:

           $_____

      (2) The *balance* in the Inventory account at January 31 was:

           $_____

      (3) The amount of costs transferred from the Inventory account to the Cost of Goods Sold account during January was:

           $_____

b   Assume that Sports Center uses a *periodic* inventory system and takes a physical inventory *only at year-end* (December 31). (*Note:* $0 may be an appropriate answer to one or more of the following questions.)

      (1) The total amount debited to the Inventory account during January was:

           $_____

      (2) The *balance* in the Inventory account at January 31 was:

           $_____

      (3) The amount of costs transferred from the Inventory account to the Cost of Goods Sold account during January was:

           $_____

CHAPTER 6   NAME_____ #_____

10-MINUTE QUIZ D   SECTION_____

Color Copy Co. is an office-supply store. The company uses a perpetual inventory system, records purchases at *net cost*, and records sales revenue at full invoice price.

Record the following transactions in the company's general journal. To conserve space, you may *omit* the written explanations that normally should accompany the entries.

July 1   Purchased four Fuji copying machines on account from Fuji Corp. Total invoice price was $2,000 per machine ($8,000 total); terms of 2/10, n/30. These machines are intended for resale.

  3   Found one of the Fuji copiers to be defective and returned it to Fuji, thus reducing the amount owed.

  9   Sold one of the Fuji copiers to Sun Realty. The sales price was $3,600, terms 5/10, n/60.

  10   Paid the remaining amount owned to Fuji Corp., less the allowable discount.

  19   Received full payment from Sun, less the allowable discount.

Date	General Journal		

SOLUTIONS TO CHAPTER 6   10-MINUTE QUIZZES

QUIZ A

1	D
2	C
3	B
4	A
5	C

QUIZ B

1	C
2	C
3	B
4	A
5	C
6	A

QUIZ C

a (1) <u>$93,000</u>   (The merchandise purchases)

(2) <u>$222,000</u> ($210,000 + $93,000 - $81,000)

(3) <u>$81,000</u> (The cost of merchandise sold)

b (1) <u>$-0-</u> (In a periodic system, merchandise purchases are debited to the ***Purchases*** account, not the Inventory account.)

(2) <u>$210,000</u> (The balance at the ***beginning*** of the month)

(3) <u>$0</u> (In a periodic system, no entries are made to transfer costs as sales occur from the Inventory account to the Cost of Goods Sold account.)

General Journal

July 1	Inventory	7,840	
	Accounts Payable (Fuji Corp.)		7,840
3	Accounts Payable (Fuji Corp).	1,960	
	Inventory		1,960
9	Accounts Receivable (Sun Realty)	3,600	
	Sales		3,600
	Cost of Goods Sold	1,960	
	Inventory		1,960
10	Accounts Payable (Fuji Corp.)	5,880	
	Cash		5,880
19	Cash	3,420	
	Sales Discounts	180	
	Accounts Receivable (Sun Realty)		3,600

Assignment Guide to Chapter 6

	Exercises	Problems						Cases					Net
	1–14	1	2	3	4	5	6	1	2	3	4	5	1
Time estimate (in minutes)	<15	35	35	20	30	30	40	35	25	25	No time	10	25
Difficulty rating	E	M	M	M	M	S	S	M	M	M	Group	E	E
Learning Objectives:													
1. Define the *operating cycle* of a merchandising company.	1, 2	✓	✓									✓	
2. Describe *subsidiary ledgers* and explain their usefulness.	3		✓				✓			✓			
3. Account for purchases and sales of merchandise in a *perpetual* inventory system.	1, 4, 6, 12	✓	✓		✓	✓	✓				✓		
4. Explain how a *period* inventory system operates.	7, 8, 12, 13						✓		✓		✓		
5. Discuss the factors to be considered in selecting an inventory system.	9, 12, 13	✓					✓				✓		
6. Define *special journals* and explain their usefulness.							✓				✓		
7. Account for additional merchandising transactions related to purchases and sales.	1, 3, 5, 10				✓	✓	✓						
8. Measure the performance of a merchandising business.	4, 5, 9, 11, 14	✓	✓	✓			✓					✓	✓

Chapter Summary

This is the first in a series of chapters analyzing major balance sheet items. Topical coverage includes cash, short term investments in marketable securities, and receivables. Accounting practices concerning these assets are often highly procedural. In order to provide a more meaningful context for the student, our treatment is organized around the theme of efficient cash management. The theme is developed from the outset with the *Business Week* article that introduces the chapter.

Discussion of cash is organized around a series of critical internal control issues. Topics include: accounting for cash over and short; use of a voucher system to foster separation of duties; preparation of the bank reconciliation; and, operation of a petty cash fund. Discussion of each topic emphasizes how the firm can achieve the objectives of efficient cash management.

The *mark-to-market* valuation of short term investments in marketable securities is the major topic of our discussion of these assets. Detailed analysis of the accounting practices relative to short term investments is deferred to a *Supplemental Topic* section. This material may be omitted without loss of continuity if so desired.

The remainder of the chapter concentrates on accounting for uncollectible accounts receivable. The allowance method is discussed in detail. Coverage is provided for both the balance sheet and income statement methods, and a brief discussion of the direct charge-off method is included. Discussion of the accounts receivable turnover ratio continues the financial statement analysis begun in an earlier chapter.

A second *Supplemental Topic* section is devoted to a detailed examination of notes receivable for those who wish to include this material.

Learning Objectives

1.   Define *financial assets* and explain their valuation in the balance sheet.

2.   Describe the objectives of cash management.

3.   Explain means of achieving *internal control* over cash transactions.

4.   Prepare a bank reconciliation and explain its purpose.

5.   Account for uncollectible accounts receivable using the *allowance* and *direct write-off* methods.

6.   Evaluate the liquidity of various financial assets.

7.   Explain how transactions discussed in this chapter affect net income and cash flows.

*8.   Account for transactions involving marketable securities.

**9.   Explain, compute, and account for the accrual of interest revenue.

Brief topical outline

     b   Other credit cards

  12 Financial analysis - see *Case in Point* (page **286**) and *Your Turn* (page **287**)

     a   Concentrations of credit risk

  13 Notes receivable and interest charges - see *Cash Effects* (page **288**)

Supplemental Topic A

D Accounting for marketable securities

  1   Purchases of marketable securities

  2   Recognition of investment revenue

  3   Sale of investments

     a   Sale at a price resulting in a gain

     b Sale at a price resulting in a loss

  4   Adjusting marketable securities to market value

     a   The mark-to-market adjustment: an illustration

     b Mark-to-market affects only the balance sheet

  5   Reporting investment transactions in the financial statements

     a   Mark-to-market and income taxes

****Supplemental Topic B***

E Notes receivable and interest revenue

  1   Nature of interest

     a   Computing interest

  2   Accounting for notes receivable

     a   Illustrative entries

     b If the maker of a note defaults - see *Case in Point* (page **295**)

     c   Discounting notes receivable

  3   The decision of whether to accrue interest

Topical coverage and suggested assignment

Class Meetings on Chapter	Topical Outline Coverage	Homework Assignment (To Be Completed Prior to Class)				
		Discussion Questions	Exercises	Problems	Cases	Internet
1	A	3, 4, 5, 6	1, 3, 5, 6	1, 2	1, 5	1
2	B	11, 12, 13	8			
3	C	17, 19, 20	9, 12, 14	3, 4		
*4	*D - *E	24, 25	*15, *16,*17	*5, *6		

* Optional assignment, time permitting.

Comments and observations

Teaching objectives for Chapter 7

Our specific teaching objectives in this chapter are to:

1   Explain the flow of financial resources among financial assets, and the valuation of those assets in the balance sheet.

2   Briefly describe the presentation of cash, cash equivalents, and restricted cash in the balance sheet.

3   Explain the objectives of *cash management*.

4   Discuss the basic internal control concepts relating to cash receipts and cash payments.

5   Explain the importance of reconciling bank accounts; illustrate the preparation of a bank reconciliation and the related entries to update the accounting records.

6   Explain the nature of investments in marketable securities, and their role in efficient cash management.

7   Discuss the application of the *"mark-to-market"* principle to marketable securities.

8   Discuss the accounting principles applicable to the valuation of accounts receivable stressing the *matching* principle.

9   Demonstrate the recognition of credit losses using allowance methods, with emphasis on the aging schedule (balance sheet) approach.

10   Illustrate write-offs and recoveries of accounts receivable when an allowance is in use.

11   Contrast the *direct write-off* method with the "allowance" method.

12   Briefly discuss various types of credit card sales, emphasizing that "bank card" sales actually are cash sales.

13   Explain why accounts receivable may be viewed as "nonproductive" assets, and identify several ways of converting receivables quickly into cash.

*14 Illustrate journal entries to record transactions arising out of investments in marketable securities.

**15   Explain and illustrate accounting for notes receivable.

New features in Chapter 7

In most respects, our coverage of cash, marketable securities, and receivables parallels that in the preceding edition. The *Your Turn* cases center on efficient cash management and accounts receivable turnover. Both of these should motivate lively class discussions.

The assignment material includes several new exercises dealing with personal use of accounting information, cash equivalents, cash management, internal control, "mark-to-market" valuation of securities, and accounts receivable turnover.

General comments

In Chapter 7, we emphasize the importance of strong internal control over cash transactions. Internal control is of special importance with respect to cash for two reasons. First, cash is the asset most susceptible to theft or embezzlement. Second, however, is that cash transactions *affect every category* of financial statement account. Thus, cash transactions *absolutely must* be recorded properly if the accounting records are to be reliable. If a company does not have adequate internal control to assure that cash receipts and cash payments are recorded properly, errors may exist virtually anywhere in the accounting records and financial statements.

The importance of properly recording cash transactions also explains our emphasis upon bank reconciliations in this chapter. A bank reconciliation brings to light most errors in recording the dollar amounts of cash receipts or cash disbursements during the period.

A continuing goal in this edition is to focus upon the use of financial accounting information not only by outsiders, but also by management. Therefore, we have supplemented our coverage of cash management with an introduction that describes the flow of funds from one form of financial asset to another over the course of the operating cycle. We highly recommend an in-class review of Exercise *12*, which makes a good point and is based on data from an actual company.

In our opinion, the FASB's adoption of the "mark-to-market" rule for short-term investments significantly enhances the usefulness of the balance sheet. We discuss Exercise *8* or *15* in class to review this accounting principle. Both exercises stress the importance of the change from the perspective of the *user* of the financial statements.

In large and small businesses alike, the accounting practices used in accounting for uncollectible accounts receivable are changing. For example, the income statement approach is now seldom used. As all accounts receivable software automatically produces an aging schedule, the income statement approach no longer provides a significant time advantage. As a result, most businesses now use the balance sheet approach in their monthly financial statements as well as in their audited annual statements.

The direct write-off method of computing uncollectible accounts expense is now the only approach allowable for income tax purposes. As a result, many small businesses, and also larger businesses in which the allowance for doubtful accounts is not material, are switching to this method for financial reporting purposes.

We want to recommend several specific Problems and Cases for use in the second and third class meetings on this chapter. Problem *4* provides efficient yet comprehensive coverage of the "balance sheet" method of accounting for receivables. Case *3* provides a good review of the accounting theory underlying this chapter, and Case *4* is an excellent "decision oriented" case relating cash flows and credit policies.

An aside The events leading up to the FASB's adoption of FASB 107 requiring the disclosure of market values of financial instruments, and FASB 115 requiring "mark-to-market" valuation constitute a fascinating case study of the importance of accounting information in a market economy. One example is provided by the virtual collapse of the thrift industry in the late eighties. Until passage of the The Depository Institutions Deregulation and Monetary Control Act of 1980, the investment and lending powers of savings and loan associations were heavily regulated. According to a 1990 SEC study, if market values had been used, the thrift industry would have recorded negative net worth of $118 billion as early as 1978. It is interesting to speculate how the public and Congress would have responded to calls for deregulation in 1980 if this market value accounting information had been available.

Another aside Estimating uncollectible accounts is one of the gray areas in financial accounting. In 1986, Miniscribe Corp. engaged in a number of questionable accounting practices prior to a large bond issue. One of these was to reduce its allowance for doubtful accounts despite the fact that its receivables had more than doubled from the prior year. This accounting decision obviously had a favorable impact on both earnings and the firm's current ratio. Students might be interested in discussing the ethical dimensions of such a decision. A fascinating account of Miniscribe's accounting machinations appears in the ***Wall Street Journal*** of May 14, 1992.

Supplemental Exercises

Business Week Exercise

Maintaining a positive cash flow is critical to the survival of any business. Kmart, a former retail giant, declared Chapter 11 bankruptcy on January 22, 2002. Refer to "Kmart's Shopping List for Survival", *Business Week*, March 15, 2002, to see how Kmart is trying to boost its cash flow. List some strategies CEO James Adamson has employed to turn Kmart around.

Group Exercise

Video rental stores carry out a large volume of small cash transactions. Make a listing of what you feel are the critical internal control concerns at such a store. When your list is complete, visit a store and through observation and interviews prepare a report in which you explain how the internal control concerns are being addressed. Explain why you feel the controls in place either are or are not adequate.

Internet Exercise

Visit the website of ADP, Inc. at www.adp.com. Access the most recent annual report and examine the balance sheet and the notes to the financial statements. What kind of transactions give rise to most of ADP's receivables? Explain how ADP discloses the magnitude of its allowance for uncollectible accounts. Why do you suppose that the allowance for uncollectible accounts does not appear in the balance sheet itself?

CHAPTER 7 NAME_____ #_____

10-MINUTE QUIZ A SECTION_____

Indicate the best answer for each question in the space provided.

> *Use the following data for questions 1 and 2.*
> At the end of the month the unadjusted trial balance of Blackhawk Company included the
> following accounts:

	Debit	Credit
Sales (75% represent credit sales)		$1,240,000
Accounts Receivable	$1,195,000	
Allowance for Doubtful Accounts....................................		13,270

_____ 1 ***Refer to the above data.*** If the income statement approach to estimating uncollectible
accounts expense is followed, and uncollectible accounts expense is estimated to be 2%
of net credit sales, the ***net realizable value*** of Blackhawk's accounts receivable at the
end of the month is:
    a $1,163,130. **b** $18,600. **c** $31,870. **d** $1,189,670.

_____ 2 ***Refer to the above data.*** If Blackhawk uses the balance sheet approach in estimating
uncollectible accounts, and aging the accounts receivable indicates the estimated
uncollectible portion to be $24,000, the ***uncollectible accounts expense*** for the month
is:
    a $24,000. **b** $10,730. **c** $37,270. **d** $156,000.

_____ 3 Which of the following items is reported in ***neither*** the income statement nor the
statement of cash flows?
    a Sale of marketable securities at a loss.
    b Sale of marketable securities at a gain.
    c Adjustment of marketable securities owned to current market value at balance
sheet date.
    d Investment of excess cash in marketable securities.

_____ 4 ***Mark-to-market*** is the balance sheet valuation standard for:
    a Investments in all financial assets.
    b Investments in marketable securities.
    c Investments in capital stock of any corporation.
    d Stockholders' equity of any publicly traded corporation.

_____ 5 Cash equivalents:
    a Include amounts of cash available through an unused line of credit.
    b Are investments in the publicly traded stocks and bonds of large corporations.
    c Are usually included in the term "cash" in the balance sheet and the statement of
cash flows.
    d Is another term for financial assets.

Shown below is a partially completed bank reconciliation for Keith Transport at August 31, as well as additional data necessary to answer the questions that follow.

KEITH TRANSPORT
Bank Reconciliation
August 31, 20__

Balance per bank statement, August 31	$26,550
Add:	
Less:	_____
Adjusted balance	$_____
Balance per depositor's records, August 31	$19,050
Add:	
Less:	_____
Adjusted balance (as above)	$_____

Additional information

a   Outstanding checks: no. 729, $1,890; no. 747, $450; no. 752, $1,215.
b   Check no. 742 (for repairs) was written for $684 but erroneously recorded in Keith's records as $486.
c   Deposits in transit, $4,140.
d   Note collected by the bank and credited to Keith's account, $9,600.
e   NSF check of C. Thomas, one of Keith's customers, $1,278.
f   Bank service charge for August, $39.

_____   1   In Keith's completed bank reconciliation at August 31, what dollar amount should be deducted from the balance per bank statement (indicated by **2** above)?
              a $1,515.   b $3,555.   c $1,317.   d $3,753.

_____   2   In Keith's completed bank reconciliation at August 31, what dollar amount should be added to the balance per depositor's records (indicated by **3** above)?
              a $4,140.   b $3,555.   c $9,600.   d $4,338.

_____   3   In Keith's completed bank reconciliation at August 31, what dollar amount should be deducted from the balance per depositor's records (indicated by **4** above)?
              a $1,317.   b $3,555.   c $3,753.   d $1,515.

_____ 4   Keith Transport keeps $500 cash on hand in addition to this checking account and has no other bank accounts or cash equivalents. What amount should appear as Cash in Keith's August 31 balance sheet?

a $27,635.   c $27,135.
b $19,650.   d   Some other amount.

_____ 5   The necessary adjustment to Keith Transport's accounting records as of August 31 includes a net:

a   Increase to Cash of $7,500.   c   Increase to Cash of $8,085.
b   Increase to Cash of $585.   d   Decrease to Cash of $198.

CHAPTER 7   NAME_____ #_____

10-MINUTE QUIZ C   SECTION_____

1   You are to complete the June 30 bank reconciliation for Moby, Inc. using the following information:

a	Outstanding checks:			c	Deposit in transit.................	$3,000
	No. 181	$ 400		d	Note collected by bank as	
	No. 184	350			Moby's agent (no	
	No. 185	275			interest)	4,000
b	Check no. 142 (for Repair			e	NSF check of I. T. Noweg...	100
	Expense) was written for $210			f	Bank service charge	50
	but erroneously recorded in					
	Moby's records as $120					
	Difference	90				

MOBY, INC.
Bank Reconciliation
June 30, 20__

Balance per bank statement, June 30	$18,100
Add:	
Less:	_____
Adjusted balance	$_____
Balance per depositor's records, June 30	$15,315
Add:	
Less:	_____
Adjusted balance (as above)	$_____

2   Give in general journal form the entry or entries necessary to correct Moby's records as of June 30. (Explanations may be omitted; one compound journal entry is acceptable.)

20__	General Journal	Debit	Credit
June 30			

CHAPTER 7   NAME_____ #_____

10-MINUTE QUIZ D   SECTION_____

1   After aging its accounts receivable at December 31, Morrison Company estimates that $21,000 of the $750,000 outstanding accounts receivable will prove uncollectible. Allowance for Doubtful Accounts has a debit balance of $2,600 prior to adjustment. In the space provided, prepare the adjusting entry required by Morrison in this situation:

Dec. 31			

2   At year-end, Laird Company applies the income statement approach in estimating uncollectible accounts expense and determines such expense to be 2% of net sales. At December 31 of the current year, accounts receivable total $900,000, and Allowance for Doubtful Accounts has a credit balance of $2,400 prior to adjustment. Net sales for the current year were $3,600,000. Compute the *net realizable value* of accounts receivable to be reported in Laird's December 31 balance sheet.

$_____

3   During the year, Misono Corporation's average accounts receivable were $495,000. The current-year income statement reported net sales of $3,712,500, uncollectible accounts expense of $247,500, and net income of $2,227,500. Using 365 days to a year, compute the average number of days Misono waits to collect its accounts receivable. (Round answer to the nearest day, if necessary.)

_____ days

Use the following for questions 4 and 5.

The Cash account in the ledger of Zane Construction shows a balance of $8,263 at September 30. The bank statement, however, shows a balance of $10,450 at the same date. The only reconciling items consist of a bank service charge of $26, outstanding checks totaling $2,965, a deposit in transit, and an error in recording check no. 529. Check no. 529 was written in the amount of $893 but was recorded as $839 in Zane's accounting records.

4   *Refer to the above data.* What is the *adjusted cash balance* in the September 30 bank reconciliation?

$_____

5   *Refer to the above data.* What is the amount of the *deposit in transit?*

$_____

SOLUTIONS TO CHAPTER 7   10-MINUTE QUIZZES

QUIZ A
1   A
2   B
3   C
4   B
5   C

QUIZ B
1   B
2   C
3   D
4   A
5   C

QUIZ C

1

MOBY, INC.
Bank Reconciliation
June 30, 20__

Balance per bank statement, June 30		$18,100
Add: Deposit in transit..		2,000
		$20,100
Less: Outstanding checks:		
No. 181..	$ 400	
No. 184..	350	
No. 185..	275	(1,025)
Adjusted balance		$19,075
Balance per depositor's records, June 30....................................		$15,315
Add: Note collected by bank as our agent		4,000
		$19,315
Less: Error in recording check no. 142	$ 90	
NSF check from I. T. Noweg	100	
Bank service charge..	50	(240)
Adjusted balance (as above)		$19,075

2

20__	General Journal	Debit	Credit
June 30	Cash	3,760	
	Repair Expense	90	
	Accounts Receivable, I. T. Noweg	100	
	Bank Service Charges	50	
	Notes Receivable		4,000

QUIZ D

1

Dec. 31	Uncollectible Accounts Expense	23,600	
	Allowance for Doubtful Accounts		23,600
	To increase allowance for doubtful accounts to $21,000.		

2

$900,000 - $74,400 ([$3,600,000 × .02] + $2,400) = $825,600.

3

Accounts receivable turnover: $3,712,500/$495,000 = 7.5 times.
Average days to collect receivables: 365 days/7.5 = 49 days (rounded to nearest day).

4

Adjusted cash balance: $8,183.
Balance per books $8,263 - $26 service charge - $54 error = $8,183 adjusted cash balance.

5

Deposit in transit: $698.
Balance per bank statement $10,450 - $2,965 outstanding checks = $7,485.
Adjusted cash balance $8,183 (from **4** above) - $7,485 = $698 deposit in transit.

Assignment Guide to Chapter 7

	Exercises	Problems						Cases					Net
	1-18	1	2	3	4	5	6	1	2	3	4	5	1
Time estimate (in minutes)	<15	40	40	25	30	60	25	25	30	30	30	30	30
Difficulty rating	E	M	M	S	M	S	E	M	M	M	M	M	M
Learning Objectives:													
1. Define financial assets and explain their valuation in the balance sheet.	2, 6, 7, 8, 9, 11, 13, 14, 15, 16, 18	√		√	√	√							√
2. Describe the objectives of cash management.	2, 3, 4, 6, 7		√		√				√	√			√
3. Explain means of achieving internal control over cash transactions.	3, 4		√					√					
4. Prepare a bank reconciliation and explain its purpose.	1, 5	√	√						√				
5. Account for uncollectible receivables using the allowance and direct write-off methods.	9, 12, 14			√	√				√	√			
6. Evaluate the liquidity of various financial assets.	10, 14, 18								√		√	√	√
7. Explain how transactions discussed in this chapter affect net income and cash flows.	11, 15, 16										√	√	
*8. Account for transactions involving marketable securities.	8, 15, 16					√			√			√	
†9. Explain, compute, and account for the accrual of interest revenue.	17						√			√			

©The McGraw-Hill Companies, Inc., 2003

Instructor's Resource Manual

8

INVENTORIES AND
THE COST OF GOODS SOLD

Chapter Summary

The chapter is a detailed introduction to the cost flow assumptions used to value inventories and measure the cost of goods sold.

Application of specific identification, average cost, FIFO and LIFO is first examined within the context of a perpetual inventory system. The impact of the flow assumption employed on income taxes is discussed in detail. The need for a physical inventory to assess inventory shrinkage is also reviewed as are the accounting procedures necessary to record inventory shrinkage. A brief presentation of lower-of-cost-or-market write downs concludes the discussion of perpetual systems.

Application of the flow assumptions within a periodic system is next explained. We also demonstrate that restatement of ending inventory by the periodic method results in the maximum tax advantage from the LIFO flow assumption.

The chapter covers a number of additional issues surrounding inventory accounting. These include: the financial statement effects of inventory errors; the retail and gross profit methods for estimating ending inventory; and, an analysis of the inventory turnover ratio. A *Supplemental Topic* on LIFO reserves is also included.

Learning Objectives

1. In a perpetual inventory system, determine the cost of goods sold using (a) *specific identification*, (b) *average cost*, (c) *FIFO*, and (d) *LIFO*. Discuss the advantages and shortcomings of each method.

2. Explain the need for taking a physical inventory.

3. Record *shrinkage losses* and other year-end adjustments to inventory.

4. In a periodic inventory system, determine the ending inventory and the cost of goods sold using (a) *specific identification*, (b) *average cost*, (c) *FIFO*, and (d) *LIFO*.

5. Explain the effects on the income statement of errors in inventory valuation.

6. Estimate the cost of goods sold and ending inventory by *gross profit* method and the *retail method*.

7. Compute the *inventory turnover rate* and explain its uses.

*8. Define a *"LIFO reserve"* and explain its implications to users of financial statements.

Brief topical outline

A The flow of inventory costs
    1 Specific identification
    2 Cost flow assumptions
    3 Average-cost method
    4 First-in, first-out method
    5 Last-in, first-out method
    6 Evaluation of the methods
        a Specific identification
        b Average cost
        c First-in, first-out
        d Last-in, first-out
    7 Do inventory methods really affect performance? - see *Cash Effects* (page **327**)
    8 The principle of ***consistency***
    9 Just-in-time (JIT) inventory system - see *Management Strategy* (page **329**) and *Case in Point* (page **329**)

B Taking a physical inventory
    1 Recording shrinkage losses
    2 LCM and other write-downs of inventory - see *Case in Point (*page **331**)
        a The lower-of-cost-or-market (LCM) rule
    3 The year-end cutoff of transactions
        a Matching revenue and the cost of goods sold
        b Goods in transit - see *Your Turn* (page **332**)
    4 Periodic inventory systems
        a Applying assumption a periodic system
        b Specific identification
        c Average cost
        d FIFO
        e LIFO - see *Case in Point* (page **334**)
        f Receiving the maximum tax benefit from the LIFO method – see *Case in Point* (page **335**)
        g Pricing the year-end inventory by computer
    5 Importance of an accurate valuation of inventory
        a Effects of an error in valuing ending inventory
        b Inventory errors affect two years - see *Case in Point* (page **336**)
        c Effects of errors in inventory valuation: a summary
    6 Techniques for estimating the cost of goods sold and the ending inventory
    7 The gross profit method
    8 The retail method - see *Case in Point* (page **339**)

C Financial analysis
   1 Inventory turnover rate - see *Cash Effects* (page **340**)
   2 Length of operating cycle – see *Your Turn* (page **340**)
   3 Accounting methods can affect analytical ratios - see *Case in Point* (page **341**) and *A Second Look* (page **341**)
Supplemental Topic
D LIFO reserves - see *Case in Point* (page **342**)
   1 The significance of a LIFO reserve
     a Comparing LIFO and FIFO inventories
     b Liquidation of a LIFO reserve - see *Case in Point* (page **342**) and *Cash Effects* (page **343**)
     c Assessing the income tax benefits of using LIFO - see *Your Turn* (page **343**)

Topical coverage and suggested assignment

Class Meetings on Chapter	Topical Outline Coverage	Homework Assignment (To Be Completed Prior to Class)				
		Discussion Questions	Exercises	Problems	Cases	Internet
1	A	2, 3, 4	2, 3	2, 3		
2	B	7, 11, 13, 17	7, 9, 10	5, 6, 7		
3	C - *D	23, 24	12, 13, *14		*3	1

Comments and observations

Teaching objectives for Chapter 8

Our specific teaching objectives in this chapter are to:

1 Explain why it is necessary for a company with an inventory to either use specific identification or adopt a "flow assumption."

2 Illustrate the "flow of costs" into the cost of goods sold account using each costing method (specific identification, average cost, FIFO, and LIFO).

3 Discuss the factors to be considered in the selection of an appropriate cost method.

4 Illustrate the recording of shrinkage losses and other year-end adjustments to inventory (excepting that in objective 6, below).

5   Illustrate the valuation of ending inventory using periodic costing procedures.

6   Explain why companies using perpetual LIFO might adjust the valuation of inventory at year-end to the amount indicated by periodic LIFO costing procedures.

7   Illustrate the gross profit and retail methods of estimating the cost of goods sold and ending inventory.

8   Identify factors which management should consider in determining the optimal size of inventory; discuss the "just-in-time" concept.

9   Discuss the purpose of computing a company's inventory turnover rate.

*10   Define a "LIFO reserve" and explain its implications to users of financial statements.

New features in Chapter 8

Our coverage of topics in this chapter is in all important respects similar to that of the preceding edition. New *Case in Point* capsules deal with JIT manufacturing systems, inventory write-downs, and the IASC position on the use of LIFO. The assignment material includes a new exercise requiring the use of an annual report to evaluate the liquidity of inventory. New requirements calling for analysis and evaluation have been added to several of the exercises, problems, and cases.

General comments

As in the previous edition, we emphasize the perpetual inventory system primarily because this is the method now in predominant use. Teaching with an emphasis on perpetual inventory systems has a number of benefits in the classroom.

Of greatest importance, a perpetual system shifts the focal point of cost assignment from ending inventory to the cost of goods sold. As a result, the names of the flow assumptions finally "mean what they say." For example, "first-in, first-out" means that the first costs are used in the cost assignment process; "last-in, first-out" means that the last costs are used. Under a periodic system, the reverse is true. (Experienced instructors will remember trying to explain to students that "first-in, first-out" actually means that the latest costs are assigned to inventory, whereas "last-in, first-out" really means the first costs are assigned.)

Not only do students more quickly grasp the concepts underlying the flow assumptions when we assume a perpetual inventory system, but they also quickly grasp the effects of using different assumptions during a period of rising prices. This enables us to emphasize the effects of different methods upon earnings, income tax considerations, and even the implications of LIFO reserves.

We use Exercise *2* to illustrate the basic cost-flow assumptions and follow it with a discussion of Exercise *11* to demonstrate the effects of using alternative methods. Exercise *12* presents a more challenging analysis of the same points. We also discuss in class such topics as "just-in-time" systems, inventory shrinkage, and the factors management should consider in determining the optimal size of a company's inventory. These discussions portray inventory as physical goods moving in and out of the business, rather than merely as a dollar amount. We find that these discussions contribute to students' interest, and also to their understanding of the importance of inventories to accountants, managers, and investors.

One of our favorite topics in this chapter is the discussion of LIFO reserves as a *Supplemental Topic.* Traditionally, few instructors have viewed LIFO reserves as an introductory topic. However, our focus upon perpetual inventory systems opens new vistas. We find that students now have a sufficient understanding of cost flows to grasp quickly the idea of a LIFO inventory becoming significantly understated over time. We are able to explain LIFO reserves, and the ramifications of "liquidating" the reserve, in about 10 or 15 minutes, using either Case *4* or the *Your Turn* case on page **338** as the basis for our discussion. We consider this discussion very useful in demonstrating why users of financial statements need an understanding of accounting concepts.

Supplemental Exercises

Business Week Exercises

"Corporate America is Clearing a Path to Recovery", *Business Week,* December 17, 2001, analyzes how the problems of excessive inventories and too much capital spending are being resolved by corporations. Explain how excessive inventories can hurt a company's bottom line.

Group Exercise

One of the most spectacular financial frauds of the 1980's involved computer peripherals manufacturer Miniscribe, Inc. Research the fraud and report on how inventory accounting by Miniscribe contributed to the production of grossly misleading financial statements. Hint: A good place to begin your research will be the Index of the *Wall Street Journal*.

Internet Exercise

Visit WalMart's website at http://www.walmart.com/ and access the annual report for 2001. Locate the balance sheet and observe that it includes a LIFO reserve. Explain what this means, and why WalMart chose to include it on the balance sheet.

CHAPTER 8   NAME_____ #_____

10-MINUTE QUIZ A   SECTION_____

Indicate the best answer for each question in the space provided.

_____   **1**   The primary purpose of an inventory flow assumption is to:
          a   Increase inventory turnover.
          b   Increase gross profit.
          c   Determine which unit costs are assigned to inventory, and which are assigned to the cost of goods sold.
          d   Minimize taxable income during periods of rising prices.

_____   **2**   During a period of steadily rising prices, which of the following inventory valuation methods is likely to result in the lowest *cost of goods sold*?
          a   LIFO.
          b   FIFO.
          c   The retail method.
          d   The gross profit method.

_____   **3**   The primary reason for the popularity of the LIFO flow assumption is that this method:
          a   Is most appropriate when each item in inventory is unique.
          b   Tends to minimize taxable income.
          c   Causes inventory to be reported at or near its current replacement cost.
          d   Reduces the amount of money "tied-up" in inventory.

_____   **4**   In a *periodic* inventory system, the cost of goods sold is determined by:
          a   Multiplying net sales for the period by a cost ratio.
          b   Journal entries made at the time of each sales transaction.
          c   Physically counting the quantities of merchandise sold each day, and determining the cost of these items at year-end.
          d   Subtracting the cost assigned to the ending inventory from the cost of goods available for sale during the period.

_____   **5**   Matrix Co. has an inventory turnover rate of 8, and an accounts receivable turnover rate of 6. Assuming 365 days in a year, the period of time required for Matrix to convert its inventory into cash through normal business operations is approximately:
          a   26 days.
          b   46 days.
          c   3.5 months.
          d   2 months.

Metro Bulb Inc. uses a perpetual inventory system. The company's beginning inventory of a particular product and its purchases during the month of January were as follows:

	Quantity	Unit Cost	Total Cost
Beginning inventory (Jan. 1)	10	$12	$120
Purchase (Jan. 15).....................................	15	13	195
Purchase (Jan. 23).....................................	5	14	70
Total...	30		$385

On January 28, Metro Bulb sells 16 units of this product. The other 14 units remain in inventory at January 31.

_____ 1   *Refer to above data.* Assuming that Metro Bulb uses the *average cost* flow assumption, the *cost of goods sold* to be recorded at January 28 is:
   a $205.   **c** $198.
   b $213.   **d**   Some other amount.

_____ 2   *Refer to above data.* Assuming that Metro Bulb uses the *LIFO* flow assumption, the *cost of goods sold* on January 28 is:
   a $205.   **c** $198.
   b $213.   **d**   Some other amount.

_____ 3   *Refer to above data.* Assuming that Metro Bulb uses the *FIFO* flow assumption, the *cost of goods sold* on January 28 is:
   a $205.   **c** $198.
   b $213.   **d**   Some other amount.

_____ 4   *Refer to above data.* Assuming that Metro Bulb uses the *LIFO* flow assumption, the 14 units of this product in inventory at January 31 have a total cost of:
   a $180.   **c** $187.
   b $172.   **d**   Some other amount.

_____ 5   *Refer to above data.* Assuming that Metro Bulb uses the *FIFO* flow assumption, the 14 units of this product in inventory at January 31 have a total cost of:
   a $180.   **c** $187.
   b $172.   **d**   Some other amount.

10 MINUTE QUIZ

CHAPTER 8   NAME_____ #_____

10-MINUTE QUIZ C   SECTION_____

Buster Supplies uses a perpetual inventory system. The company's beginning inventory of a particular product and its purchases during the month of January were as follows:

	Quantity	Unit Cost	Total Cost
Beginning inventory (Jan. 1)	50	$10	$ 500
Purchase (Jan. 10)..	25	11	275
Purchase (Jan. 22)..	25	13	325
Total	100		$1,100

On January 25, Buster sells 60 units of this product. The other 40 units remain in inventory at January 31.

a   Determine the *cost of goods sold* using each of the following flow assumptions:

   (1) LIFO $_____

   (2) FIFO $_____

   (3) Average cost $_____

b   Determine the cost of the 40 units *in inventory* at January 31 using each of the following flow assumptions:

   (1) LIFO $_____

   (2) FIFO $_____

   (3) Average cost $_____

CHAPTER 8   NAME_____ #_____

10-MINUTE QUIZ D   SECTION_____

Monitor Systems uses a periodic inventory system. The beginning inventory of a particular product, and the purchases during the current year, were as follows:

Jan.	1	Beginning inventory.........................	50	units @	$102	=	$ 5,100
Mar.	8	Purchase	40	units @	$110	=	4,400
Aug.	11	Purchase	80	units @	$120	=	9,600
Oct.	23	Purchase	30	units @	$130	=	3,900
		Total available for sale...................................	200	units			$23,000

At December 31, the ending inventory of this product consisted of **55** units.

Using periodic costing procedures, determine (1) cost of the year-end inventory and, (2) cost of goods sold relating to this product under each of the following flow assumptions:

		(1) **Inventory** **at Dec. 31**	**(2)** **Cost of** **Goods Sold**
a	Average cost	$_____	$_____
b	First-in, first-out	$_____	$_____
c	Last-in, first-out	$_____	$_____

SOLUTIONS TO CHAPTER 8   10-MINUTE QUIZZES

QUIZ A

1   C
2   B
3   B
4   D
5   C

QUIZ B

1   A
2   B
3   C
4   B
5   C

QUIZ C

a   Cost of goods sold
    (1) $700   (25 @ $13) + (25 @ $11) + (10 @ $10)
    (2) $610   (50 @ $10) + (10 @ $11)
    (3) $660   ($1,100/100) x 60

b   Inventory at Jan. 31:
    (1) $400   ($1,100 - $700)
    (2) $490   ($1,100 - $610)
    (3) $440   (40 @ $11)

QUIZ D

a   Average cost:

Inventory	$6,325	[55 @ ($23,000 ÷ 200)]
Cost of goods sold	$16,675	($23,000 - $6,325)

b   First-in, first-out:

Inventory	$6,900	(30 @ $130) + (25 @ $120)
Cost of goods sold	$16,100	($23,000 - $6,900)

c   Last-in, first-out:

Inventory	$5,650	(50 @ $102) + (5 @ $110)
Cost of goods sold	$17,350	($23,000 - $5,650)

Assignment Guide to Chapter 8

	Exercises	Problems								Cases				Net
	1-15	1	2	3	4	5	6	7	8	1	2	3	4	1
Time estimate (in minutes)	>15	40	40	25	30	60	25	25	35	25	30	30	25	40
Difficulty rating	E	M	M	S	M	S	E	M	M	M	M	M	M	E
Learning Objectives:														
1. In a perpetual inventory system, determine the cost of goods sold using (a) specific identification, (b) average cost, (c) FIFO, and (d) LIFO. Discuss the advantages and shortcomings of each method.	1, 2, 3, 4, 11, 12	√	√						√					
2. Explain the need for taking a physical inventory.	1, 5				√			√						
3. Record shrinkage losses and other year-end adjustments to inventory.	1, 6				√			√			√			
4. In a periodic inventory system, determine the ending inventory and the cost of goods sold using (a) specific identification (b) average cost, (c) FIFO, and (d) LIFO.	1, 7			√		√								
5. Explain the effects on the income statement of errors in inventory valuation.	1, 8	√					√			√			√	
6. Estimate the cost of goods sold and ending inventory by the gross profit method and by the retail method.	1, 9, 10							√		√				
7. Compute the inventory turnover rate and explain its uses.	1, 11, 12, 13, 15								√					√
*8. Define a "LIFO reserve" and explain its implications to users of financial statements.	1, 14											√		

Chapter Summary

The material on plant assets is organized into sections for tangible assets, intangible assets, and natural resources.

For all three categories of plant assets the chapter focuses on three accountable events: (1) acquisition, (2) allocation of the acquisition cost to expense over the asset's lifetime, and (3) sale or disposal. In determining the cost of a plant asset, careful attention is paid to distinguishing between capital and revenue expenditures. Special considerations surrounding the acquisition of land, existing structures, and land improvements are briefly discussed, as is the allocation of lump-sum purchases.

A considerable amount of attention is paid to depreciation. Before discussing various methods of calculating periodic depreciation, a conceptual introduction explains that depreciation is simply the process of allocating a recorded cost and does not represent an accounting effort to establish the market value of a plant asset. At this point in the course, the student is already aware of the calculation of straight-line depreciation and the adjusting entry to record the expense. Accounting for residual values and dealing with fractional periods completes the discussion from prior chapters. Accelerated depreciation is introduced using the declining balance method for illustration. Additional accelerated methods are discussed in a *Supplemental Topic*.

Accounting for the disposal of plant assets requires a journal entry to remove both the original recorded cost of the asset and the accumulated depreciation. The chapter deals with sales for cash, trade-ins, and scrapping worthless equipment. The calculation of gain or loss is illustrated only for financial statement purposes. Trade-in transactions are treated only briefly at an introductory level.

A wide variety of intangible assets including trademarks, patents, copyrights, and franchises is discussed, but only goodwill is treated in detail. The difficulty of objectively estimating goodwill is explained as the reason that this asset is only recorded when purchased.

The brief discussion of natural resources parallels that for equipment. We emphasize that depletion is first recorded as inventory and charged to expense as the material is sold.

Learning Objectives

1. Determine the cost of plant assets.

2. Distinguish between *capital expenditures* and *revenue expenditures*.

3. Compute depreciation by the *straight-line* and *declining-balance* methods.

4. Account for disposals of plant assets.

5. Explain the nature of intangible assets, including *goodwill.*

6. Account for the *depletion* of natural resources.

7. Explain the cash effects of transactions involving plant assets.

*8. Account for depreciation using methods other than straight-line or declining-balance.

Brief topical outline

A Acquisition of plant assets
   1 Determining cost: an example
   2 Some special considerations
      a Land
      b Land improvements
      c Buildings
      d Equipment
      e Allocation of a lump-sum purchase - see *Your Turn* (page **370**)
   3 Capital expenditures and revenue expenditures
B Depreciation
   1 Allocating the cost of plant and equipment over the years of use
      a Depreciation is not a process of valuation - see *Cash Effects* (page **372**)
      b Book value
   2 Causes of depreciation
      a Physical deterioration
      b Obsolescence - see *Case in Point* (page *373*)
   3 Methods of computing depreciation
      a The straight-line method -see *Your Turn* (page *375*)
      b Depreciation for fractional periods
      c The declining-balance method
      d Double-declining-balance
      e 150%-declining-balance
   4 Which depreciation methods do most businesses use?
      a The difference in depreciation methods: are they "real"? -see *Cash Effects* (page **378**) and *Your Turn* (page **379**)
   5 Financial statement disclosures
      a Estimates of useful life and residual value
      b The principle of consistency
      c Revision of estimated useful lives
   6 The impairment of plant assets - see *Case in Point* (page **380**)
C Disposal of plant and equipment
   1 Gains and losses on disposals of plant and equipment - see *Case in Point* (page **381**)
      a Disposal at a price above book value
      b Disposal at a price below book value
   2 Trading in used assets for new ones

D Intangible assets

    1   Characteristics

    2   Operating expenses versus intangible assets

    3   Amortization

    4   Goodwill - see *Case in Point* (page **386**)

    5   Patents

    6   Trademarks and trade names

    7   Franchises

    8   Copyrights

    9   Other intangibles and deferred charges

    10   Research and development (R & D) costs

E Financial analysis

F Natural resources

    1   Accounting for natural resources

        a   Depreciation of buildings and equipment closely related to natural resources

    2   Depreciation, amortization, and depletion--a common goal

G Plant transactions and the statement of cash flows - see *Cash Effects* (page **390**)

    1   Noncash investing activities – see *A Second Look* (page **390**)

Supplemental Topic

H Other depreciation methods

    1   The units-of-output method

    2   MACRS

    3   Sum-of-the-years' digits

    4   Decelerated depreciation methods

    5   Depreciation methods in use: a survey

Topical coverage and suggested assignment

Class Meetings on Chapter	Topical Outline Coverage	Homework Assignment (To Be Completed Prior to Class)				
		Discussion Questions	Exercises	Problems	Cases	Internet
1	A - B	4, 5, 7, 8	2, 3, 4	1, 2, 3	1	
2	C - D	17, 18, 21, 22	8, 9	4, 5	3	1
3	E -*H		11, 13, 14	6		

Comments and observations

Teaching objectives for Chapter 9

This chapter covers accounting for plant assets, including acquisition, depreciation, and disposal. Also included in the chapter are accounting for intangible assets and brief coverage of natural resources. Our objectives in presenting this material are to:

1 Describe plant assets as a "stream of services" to be received by the business entity.

2 Distinguish between capital expenditures and revenue expenditures.

3 Explain and illustrate depreciation as a technique for allocating costs.

4 Explain and illustrate the mechanics of the depreciation methods discussed in the chapter.

5 Explain and illustrate accounting for disposals of plant assets, including "like-kind" exchanges.

6 Explain the nature of intangible assets.

7 Discuss techniques for estimating the value of the goodwill possessed by a successful business.

8 Explain and illustrate depletion; relate depreciation, amortization, and depletion to the matching principle.

*9 Discuss the determination of depreciation expense under the units-of-output and sum-of-the-years' digits methods.

New features in Chapter 9

In general terms, our coverage of plant assets is unchanged from the previous edition. The prior coverage of MACRS has been substantially reduced. Several new *Case in Point* capsules have been added to illustrate obsolescence, gains and losses on asset dispositions, research and development, and the purchase of goodwill. The assignment material includes new exercises concerning personal use of accounting information, ethical issues, and recording goodwill.

General comments

Some students have difficulty in identifying the types of expenditures included in the cost of an asset, and in distinguishing between capital expenditures and revenue expenditures. We recommend an in-class review of Discussion Questions *5* and *6* and of Exercise *2* to clarify these points.

The most important topic in this chapter is depreciation. Perhaps the greatest challenge in explaining depreciation is to dispel the idea that depreciation represents a decline in market value. Students are familiar with the term ***depreciation*** as it relates to the market value of an automobile. Discussion Question *9* and the diagram on page *365* are both designed to stress the idea that depreciation is a cost allocation process, not a valuation process.

We recommend discussing in class the extent to which depreciation is based upon judgments (estimates), and the roles of management and auditors in making and evaluating these judgments. Our *Your Turn* case on page *364* can be used to stimulate this discussion. The one form of depreciation calculation that requires no judgment or estimates is that required for income tax purposes under MACRS. We stress that different depreciation methods are typically used for financial reporting purposes and for income tax purposes. Exercise *5* and Case *3* emphasize these points. Problem *3* is a comprehensive review of the differences among depreciation methods.

In discussing intangible assets, we place greater emphasis upon the limitations of financial reporting than upon simple mechanics such as amortization over 40 years. Informed users of financial statements should recognize that a business may have intangible assets of immense economic value which do not even appear on the balance sheet, either because they were developed internally or because they have long since been amortized. Examples include the Coca-Cola trademark and the brand names "Kleenex" and "Scotch Tape."

On the other hand, the presence of an intangible on the balance sheet merely means that a cost was incurred, not that an asset necessarily exists. This is especially true of goodwill, an "asset" for which many companies greatly overpaid in the 1980s wave of corporate takeovers. This point is made in Discussion Question *20*, which we always review in class.

Caution: In discussing such issues as differences between recorded values and economic values, we consider it important not to downplay the relevance and usefulness of financial statements. Actually, financial statements and the related disclosures provide an informed reader with many clues as to resources which may have economic values significantly different from the recorded amounts. Many accounting numbers should not be taken at face value; the informed decision makers should look to the accounting policies and facts which underlie the numbers.

We view accounting for natural resources and depletion as optional topics in the introductory accounting course. Basically, these topics consist of applying units-of-output depreciation within a specific industry setting. If the topic is discussed in class, we would stress the difficulty in estimating the original quantity of the natural resource at the site.

These estimates are made by professional geologists and other specialists with expertise in fields other than accounting.

Supplemental Exercises

Business Week Exercise

In "Can Uncle Sam Move the Bottom Line?", *Business Week*, November 19, 2001, the author reports on the attempt of Congress to pass legislation to boost corporate cash flow. The legislation would offer companies accelerated depreciation on their capital spending and cut corporate tax payments by as much as $39 billion in 2001. How would accelerated depreciation lower corporate tax payments and provide corporations funding for capital investments?

Group Exercise

Access the Internal Revenue website www.irs.gov and search for MACRS Tables. Choose one column from the MACRS table for 5-year property using the half-year convention. Prepare a presentation for the class demonstrating how the percentage allowances for depreciation in this table were determined.

Internet Exercise

Obtain Exxon Mobil's most recent annual report from the company website www.exxonmobil.com Research the footnotes, balance sheet, and income statement and describe the information you find regarding depletion.

10 MINUTE QUIZ

CHAPTER 9   NAME_____ #_____

10-MINUTE QUIZ A   SECTION_____

Indicate the best answer for each question in the space provided.

> *Use the following data for independent questions 1 and 2.*
> On March 12, 2000, Duo, Inc. acquired a melting equipment for $40,000. The estimated life of the equipment is 8 years, with an estimated residual value of $8,000.

_____ 1 ***Refer to above data.*** In its financial statements, Duo uses straight-line depreciation with the half-year convention. The ***book value*** of the equipment at December 31, 2001, will be:
   a $30,000.   **b** $36,000.   **c** $34,000.   **d** Some other amount.

_____ 2 ***Refer to above data.*** In its financial statements, Duo uses the MACRS accelerated rates. The equipment is 5-year property; the MACRS depreciation rates are 20% in the year of purchase and 32% in the following year. The *tax basis* of the equipment at December 31, 2001, will be:
   a $15,360.   **b** $20,800.   **c** $19,200.   **d** Some other amount.

_____ 3 Moo Dairy sold a delivery truck for cash of $8,200. The original cost of the truck was $25,000, and a loss of $2,000 was recognized on the sale. The ***accumulated depreciation*** at the date of sale must have been:
   a $18,800.   **b** $10,200.   **c** $3,900.   **d** $14,800.

_____ 4 Dnet Corporation purchases Hardlock Company's entire business for $3,200,000. The fair market value of Hardlock's net identifiable assets is $2,900,000.
   a Hardlock should record goodwill of $300,000.
   b Dnet paid $300,000 for goodwill generated by Hardlock.
   c Dnet should charge the $300,000 excess paid for Hardlock Company directly to expense.
   d Hardlock should record amortization over a period not to exceed 40 years.

_____ 5 Throughout the current year, Telplace Company treated sales taxes paid on purchases of plant assets as revenue expenditures. As a result, the current year's:
   a Net income is overstated.
   b Revenue is overstated.
   c Depreciation expense is understated.
   d None of the above; payments of sales taxes ***should*** be treated as revenue expenditures.

CHAPTER 9 NAME_____ #_____

10-MINUTE QUIZ B SECTION_____

Indicate the best answer for each question in the space provided.

Use the following data for the five independent questions which follow:
On May 5, 2000, Duadal purchased a machine for $50,000. The estimated life of the machine was 10 years, with an estimated residual value of $10,000. The service life in terms of "output" is estimated at 8,000 hours of operation.

_____ 1   *Refer to the above data.* Assume Duadal uses *straight-line* depreciation with the half-year convention. Depreciation expense to be recognized in 2000 (the year of purchase) is:
    a $5,000.   **b** $4,000.   **c** $2,000.   **d** Some other amount.

_____ 2   *Refer to the data above.* Assume Duadal uses double-declining-balance depreciation with the half-year convention. Depreciation expense to be recognized in 2001 (the second year of ownership) is:
    a $4,000.   **b** $5,000.   **c** $9,000.   **d** Some other amount.

_____ 3   *Refer to the data above.* Assume Duadal uses *150%*-declining-balance depreciation with the half-year convention. Depreciation expense to be recognized in 2000 (the year of purchase) is:
    a $6,000.   **b** $3,750.   **c** $7,500.   **d** Some other amount.

_____ 4   *Refer to the data above.* Assume Duadal uses the units-of-output method, and that the machine was in operation for 1,000 hours in 2000 and 1,800 hours in 2001. The book value of the machine on December 31, 2001, is:
    a $25,000.   **b** $36,000.   **c** $40,000.   **d** Some other amount.

_____ 5   *Refer to the data above.* For income tax purposes, Duadal uses MACRS. The machine is classified as 7-year property, and the depreciation rates for the first two years of ownership are 14.29% and 24.49%. The *tax basis* of the machine at December 31, 2001, is:
    a $20,610.   **b** $19, 380.   **c** $30,610.   **d** Some other amount.

10 MINUTE QUIZ

On April 8, year 1, Playland purchased a Ferris wheel for $100,000. The estimated life of the Ferris wheel was 10 years, with an estimated residual value of $20,000. The service life in terms of "output" is estimated at 20,000 hours of operation.

Compute the depreciation on this Ferris wheel in year 1 and year 2 using the following methods.

		Year 1	**Year 2**
a	Straight-line (with half-year convention)	$_____	$_____
b	200%-declining-balance (with half-year convention)	$_____	$_____
c	150%-declining-balance (with half-year convention)	$_____	$_____
d	Units-of-output method (hours of operation: 1,200 in year 1, 2,500 in year 2)	$_____	$_____
e	MACRS (a Ferris wheel is classified as 7-year property; a rate table shows a depreciation rate of 14.29% for the year of acquisition, and 24.49% for the following year)	$_____	$_____

CHAPTER 9 NAME_____ #_____

10-MINUTE QUIZ D SECTION_____

Outlaw Farms, a breeder of racehorses, paid $216,000 cash for a prize-winning stallion on January 1, year 1. The stallion is depreciated on a straight-line basis, with depreciation for partial years rounded to the nearest month. Estimated useful life was nine years, with no residual value. After owning the animal for six years and five months, Outlaw Farms sold the stallion on May 31, year 7, for cash of $50,000. Depreciation had last been recorded on December 31, year 6.

a Compute to the nearest full month depreciation for the fractional period from January 1 to May 31 of year 7. $_____

b Compute the book value of the stallion at May 31, year 7, the date of sale. $_____

c Compute the gain or loss on the sale of the stallion. $_____ (gain/loss)

d In the space provided below, prepare the journal entry to record the sale of the stallion on May 31, year 7. (Use "Breeding Stock" as the title of the asset account. Assume that depreciation to date of sale already has been recorded.)

Year 7	General Journal		
May 31			

Computations

SOLUTIONS TO CHAPTER 9   10-MINUTE QUIZZES

QUIZ A

1   C
2   C
3   D
4   B
5   C

QUIZ B

1   C
2   C
3   B
4   B
5   C

QUIZ C

		Year 1	Year 2
a	Straight-line	$ 4,000	$ 8,000

       Year 1: [($100,000 - $20,000) x 1/10 x 1/2]
       Year 2: ($80,000 x 1/10)

		Year 1	Year 2
b	200%-declining-balance	$10,000	$18,000

       Year 1: ($100,000 x 20% x 1/2)
       Year 2: [($100,000 - $10,000) x 20%]

		Year 1	Year 2
c	150%-declining-balance	$ 7,500	$13,875

       Year 1: ($100,000 x 15% x 1/2)
       Year 2: [($100,000 - $7,500) x 15%]

		Year 1	Year 2
d	*Units-of-output	$ 4,800	$10,000

       Year 1: [($100,000 - $20,000) x 1,200/20,000]
       Year 2: [($100,000 - $20,000) x 2,500/20,000]

		Year 1	Year 2
e	*MACRS (7-year property)	$ 14,290	$24,490

       Year 1: ($100,000 X 14.29%)
       Year 2: ($100,000 X 24.49%)

QUIZ D

a $10,000

b $62,000

c $12,000 loss

d

Year 7	General Journal		
May 31	Loss on Sale of Breeding Stock	12,000	
	Cash	50,000	
	Accumulated Depreciation, Breeding Stock	154,000	
	Breeding Stock		216,000
	To record sale of stallion at price below book		
	value.		

Computations

a   Depreciation for the five months ended May 31, year 7
[($216,000 cost ÷ 9 years) x 5/12] ....   <u>$ 10,000</u>

b   Book value of the stallion at May 31, year 7:
       Original cost $216,000
       Depreciation for 6 years (year 1 through year 6)
       ($216,000 ÷ 9) x 6 years $144,000
       Depreciation for 5 months in year 7 (see part **a**) ....   <u>10,000</u>
       Accumulated depreciation to May 31, year 7 ....   <u>(154,000)</u>
         Book value of stallion at May 31, year 7 ....   <u>$ 62,000</u>

c   Loss on sale of the stallion:
       Sales price $50,000 - $62,000 book value ....   <u>$ 12,000</u> loss

Assignment Guide to Chapter 9

	Exercises	Problems						Cases				Net
	1-14	1	2	3	4	5	6	1	2	3	4	1
Time estimate (in minutes)	<15	40	40	25	30	60	25	25	30	30	30	25
Difficulty rating	E	M	M	S	M	S	E	M	M	M	M	M
Learning Objectives:												
1. Determine the cost of plant assets.	2, 10, 14	√		√					√			
2. Distinguish between capital expenditures and revenue expenditures.	1, 2	√		√							√	√
3. Compute depreciation by the straight-line and declining-balance methods.	1, 3, 5, 6, 14	√	√	√				√		√		
4. Account for disposals of plant assets.	4, 7, 9		√	√	√							
5. Explain the nature of intangible assets, including goodwill.	8, 10, 12					√					√	
6. Account for the depletion of natural resources.	11						√					
7. Explain the cash effects of transactions involving plant assets.	4, 9, 12											
*8. Account for depreciation using methods other than straight-line or declining-balance.	13									√		

Chapter Summary

At the outset, the chapter distinguishes between current and long-term liabilities before addressing the accounting issues surrounding each category.

Among current liabilities, notes payable and payroll related costs are analyzed in detail. Journal entries are introduced to record the issuance of a note, the accrual of interest expense, and the payment of interest and principal. Payroll costs such as FICA and Medicare taxes, unemployment insurance, workers' compensation, and the employer's share of benefits are explained and contrasted with other amounts withheld from the employees' paychecks. A number of other current liabilities with which the student is already familiar are reviewed in brief.

Long-term liabilities are introduced using installment notes payable. An example of an amortization schedule illustrates the allocation of installment payments between interest expense and principal reduction. The amortization table serves as the basis for preparing journal entries relative to the note, and is also used to demonstrate that the portion of principal scheduled to be paid in the next 12 months is classified as a current liability.

Bonds payable are discussed in some detail with emphasis on the nature and advantages of bond financing. Although accounting treatment is limited to bonds issued at par, a number of advanced topics are covered including issuance between interest payment dates, price fluctuations after issuance, and early retirement. Bonds sold at a discount or premium are examined in a *Supplemental Topic* section. Other long-term liabilities introduced include leases, pensions and other post-retirement costs, and deferred income taxes. Estimated liabilities, commitments, and contingencies are discussed as a *Supplemental Topic*.

The chapter concludes with an analysis of the interest coverage ratio and financial leverage. This discussion emphasizes how creditors use accounting data to evaluate the safety of their claims.

Learning Objectives

1.   Define *liabilities* and distinguish between current and long-term liabilities.

2.   Account for notes payable and interest expense.

3.   Describe the costs relating to payrolls.

4.   Prepare an amortization table allocating payments between interest and principal.

5.   Describe corporate bonds and explain the tax advantage of debt financing.

6. Account for bonds issued at a discount or premium.

7. Explain the concept of present value as it relates to bond prices.

8. Explain how estimated liabilities, loss contingencies, and commitments are disclosed in financial statements.

9. Evaluate the safety of creditors' claims.

*10 Understand reporting issues related to leases, postretirement benefits, and deferred taxes.

*Supplemental Topic, "Special Types of Liabilities."

Brief topical outline

A The nature of liabilities
  1 Distinction between debt and equity – see *Management Strategy & Financial Reporting* (page **410**)
  2 Many liabilities bear interest
  3 Estimated liabilities
B Current liabilities
  1 Accounts payable
  2 Notes payable
  3 The current portion of long-term debt
  4 Accrued liabilities
  5 Payroll liabilities
    a Payroll taxes and mandated costs
    b Other payroll-related costs
    c Amounts withheld from employees' pay
  6 Unearned revenue - see *Your Turn* (page **415**)
C Long-term liabilities
  1 Maturing obligations intended to be refinanced – see *Case in Point* (page **415**)
  2 Installment notes payable
    a Allocating installment payments between interest and principal
    b Preparing an amortization table - see *Cash Effects* (page **417**)
    c Using an amortization table
    d The current portion of long-term debt
  3 Bonds payable
    a What are bonds?
    b The issuance of bonds payable
    c Transferability of bonds
    d Quoted market prices

Topical coverage and suggested assignment

Class Meetings on Chapter	Topical Outline Coverage	Homework Assignment (To Be Completed Prior to Class)				
		Questions	Exercises	Problems	Cases	Internet
1	A - B	1, 3, 4, 5	5	2, 3		
2	C - D	11, 12, 14, 15	2, 3, 6, 8, 9	1, 4, 5	2	1
3	E - *H	21, 22, 23, 24	11, 12, 14		3	

Comments and observations

Teaching objectives for Chapter 10

In presenting the broad topic of liabilities, our teaching objectives in this chapter are to:

1 Define liabilities. Distinguish between liabilities and owners' equity.

2 Distinguish between current and long-term liabilities (including classification of the current portions of long-term debt and of short-term liabilities expected to be refinanced on a long-term basis).

3 Account for notes payable when interest is stated separately.

4 Explain the nature of payroll liabilities including payroll taxes and other mandated costs.

5 Explain the purpose of an amortization table. Illustrate the preparation and use of such a table in the context of an installment note payable.

6 Discuss the characteristics of corporate bonds including their tax advantages, and the basic journal entries to record their issuance, payment of interest, and redemption.

7 Explain the nature of bonds issued at a discount or premium.

8 Introduce the concept of present value and its relationship to bond prices.

9 Distinguish between capital leases and operating leases and briefly explain their accounting treatment.

10 Introduce other long-term liabilities including pensions, post-retirement benefits, and deferred taxes. Describe the presentation of these items in the financial statements.

11 Describe the cash effects of transactions involving liabilities.

12 Explain the usefulness of the debt ratio and the interest coverage ratio.

*13 Explain the nature of estimated liabilities, loss contingencies, and commitments. Describe the presentation of these items in financial statements.

New features in Chapter 10

The coverage of liabilities is substantially the same as in our previous edition. New *Case in Point* capsules have been introduced dealing with ethical issues and international reporting requirements. The assignment material includes a large number of revised exercises.

General comments

Chapter 10 opens with a general discussion of the nature of current liabilities. We recommend Problem *1* to distinguish between current and contingent liabilities, and to show that liabilities relate to past, rather than future, transactions.

What actually constitutes a "liability" is not a cut-and-dried issue, either for introductory accounting students, or in accounting practice. Hence, we always review in class an assignment such as Exercise *4* and/or Case *2*. These assignments address the nature and classification of liabilities, and of obligations that do *not* qualify as "liabilities." We believe that if students understand the concepts involved in these assignments, they have acquired a good working knowledge of how various types of obligations are reported and disclosed in financial statements.

In discussing the general nature of liabilities, we point out that only interest that has accrued through the balance sheet date is a liability. No liability currently exists with respect to interest charges applicable to *future* periods. This concept provides the foundation for accounting for notes payable.

We devote little class time to payroll taxes. We do explain that taxes *withheld* from employees are current liabilities of the employer, but do not increase the overall cost of having employees on the payroll (except for administration costs). On the other hand, payroll taxes *levied upon the employer* increase the cost of employing a work force to an amount greater than the wages and salaries expense. In view of the various current proposals for financing health care, this has become a particularly important point.

We also devote little class time to bonds payable. The basic entries concerning a bond issue—issuance, interest payments, and retirements—may be illustrated quickly by reviewing an assignment such as Exercise *8* or Problem *5*.

We recommend against spending time in the introductory course discussing bond discounts or premiums. These topics are overly complex, consume great amounts of classroom time, and are simply *not significant* in today's business environment. Our coverage in the *Supplemental Topic* section is limited to explaining *why* bonds might be issued at a discount or premium, whether amortization of the discount or premium increases or reduces interest expense, and that the dollar amounts are normally immaterial.

Many corporations have recorded the one time charge for post-retirement benefits. We have therefore commented upon the significance of these unfunded liabilities and their cash flow effects. A *Case in Point* addresses the magnitude of this problem and raises the question of whether or not a company's future cash flows from operations will be sufficient to pay these obligations.

Loss contingencies are of vital importance but can be covered quickly as the topic generally does not involve computations or entries in the accounting records. We highly recommend an in-class review of Case *4* to give students "a feel" for what types of loss contingencies should be accrued, disclosed, or ignored. Examples of critically important loss contingencies abound, as indicated in the *Asides* below:

An aside We like to use a few "real world" examples to indicate the potential impact of loss contingencies. For example, the Texas State Courts awarded *Pennzoil* an $11 billion judgment against *Texaco* for *Texaco's* alleged "improper actions" in outbidding *Pennzoil* for the acquisition of *Getty Oil.* This judgment forced *Texaco*, one of the world's largest and most profitable oil companies, to seek the protection of the Bankruptcy Court under Chapter 11 of the Bankruptcy Code. During the following year, *Texaco* emerged from Chapter 11 when this $11 billion loss contingency was settled for approximately $3 billion.

The large pharmaceutical company *A. H. Robbins* was forced into bankruptcy by product liability suits, brought against the company by users of the Dalkon Shield, an intrauterine birth control device.

In most cases, the footnotes to the companies' financial statements disclose the nature of the pending litigation long before a company is forced into bankruptcy. However, it remains for the reader of the financial statements to evaluate the financial risk associated with the pending litigation.

Supplemental Exercises

Business Week Exercise

In "Why Junk Bonds Suddenly Look Good," *Business Week,* April 8, 2002, Robert Barker offers advice for buying junk funds and explains how the economy affects junk bond prices. What are junk bonds and how are they different from traditional bonds?

Group Exercise

Current liabilities are defined as obligations that will be paid from current assets. As a result creditors and potential creditors are keenly interested in the relationship between a company's current assets and is current liabilities. This relationship is often measured by dividing current assets by current liabilities to produce what is called the *current ratio*. The ratio shows how many dollars of current assets are available for each dollar of current liabilities. Clearly, the larger the ratio the more secure are the claims of short-term creditors.

Choose a number of companies and using their annual reports, compute the current ratio for each. Based on your results, discuss how secure the claims of these companies' short term creditors seem to be.

Internet Exercise

1.   Obtain the annual report of the Harley Davidson Company either from its website www.harley-davidson.com or from the SEC's EDGAR site. Read the footnote regarding postretirement health benefits and describe the information you find.

2.   It is widely appreciated that the Federal Reserve System controls interest rates in the United States. Visit www.federalreserve.gov and write a short report on the history of the Federal Reserve Board.

Indicate the best answer for each question in the space provided.

On November 30, 2000, Summer Food purchased two trucks for a total of $60,000, issuing a one-year, 8% note payable, all due at maturity. The interest on this loan is stated separately.

_____   1   ***Refer to the above data.*** The December 31, 2000, adjusting entry for this note includes:
a   A credit to Cash for $800.
b   A credit to Interest Payable for $4,800.
c   A credit to Interest Payable for $800.
d   A credit to Interest Payable for $400.

_____   2   ***Refer to the above data.*** The total liability related to this note reported in Summer Food's ***December 31, 2000,*** balance sheet is:
a $60,000.   b $64,800.   c $60,400.   d $60,800.

_____   3   ***Refer to the above data.*** What is the amount of interest expense Summer Food's recognizes on this note in ***2001***?
a $400.   b $4,800.   c $4,400.   d $800.

_____   4   ***Refer to the above data.*** How much must Summer Food pay the lender upon maturity of this note?
a $60,400.   b $60,000.   c $64,400.   d $64,800.

_____   5   ***Refer to the above data.*** The liability for this loan as of December 31, 2000:
a   Is equal to its maturity value.
b   Is equal to the book value of the two trucks that were acquired in exchange.
c   Is classified as a long-term liability, since it was used to acquire noncurrent assets.
d   Is classified as a long-term liability if Summer Food has the intent and ability to refinance by taking out a new loan not due for several years.

Shown below is a summary of the annual payroll data of Robbins Co.:

Wages and salaries expense (gross pay)		$2,000,000
Amounts withheld form employees' pay:		
Income taxes	$160,000	
Social Security and Medicare	$150,000	310,000
Payroll taxes expense:		
Social Security and Medicare	$150,000	
Unemployment taxes	48,000	198,000
Workers' compensation premiums		120,000
Group health insurance premiums (paid by employer)		242,000
Contributions to employees pension plan (paid by		
employer and fully funded)		140,000
Cost of other postretirement benefits:		
Funded	$90,000	
Unfunded	120,000	210,000

_____ 1 *Refer to the above data.* Robbins Company's total payroll-related expense for the year is:
    a $2,000,000. **b** $3,220,000. **c** $2,790,000. **d** $2,910,000.

_____ 2 *Refer to the above data.* Compute the company's *cash outlays* during the year for payroll-related costs. Assume short-term obligations such as insurance premiums and payroll taxes have been paid.
    a $2,480,000. **b** $2,790,000. **c** $1,690,000. **d** $3,220,000.

_____ 3 *Refer to the above data.* The annual "take-home-pay" of Robbins' employees is:
    a $2,230,000. **b** $2,000,000. **c** $1,690,000. **d** $2,592,000.

_____ 4 *Refer to the above data.* Amounts paid during the year to a pension fund total:
    a $140,000. **b** $350,000. **c** $230,000. **d** None of above.

_____ 5 *Refer to the above data.* When a company has a fully funded pension plan:
    a The dollar amounts paid to retirees are less than the amounts recognized as pension expense by the employer.
    b Pension expense is equal to the cash payments made to retirees during the current period.
    c No pension liability is recognized in the balance sheet.
    d It does not use the services of a trustee to operate the pension plan.

Tile Industries received authorization on December 31, year 1, to issue $10,000,000 face value of 8%, 10-year bonds. The interest payment dates are June 30 and December 31. All the bonds were issued at par, plus accrued interest, April 1, year 2. The bonds are callable by Tile Industries at any time at 102.

1   Prepare the journal entry to record *issuance* of the bonds on *April 1, year 2.*

2   Prepare the journal entry to record the first semiannual interest payment on the bonds at *June 30, year 2.*

3   What is the amount of *bond interest expense* that appears in Tile's year 2 income statement relating to these bonds?

        $_____

4   What is the amount of accrued *bond interest expense* that appears in Tile's balance sheet at December 31, year 2, with respect to these bonds?

        $_____

5   Tile exercises the call provision and retires *one-half* of the bond issue on July, 1, year 4. Prepare the journal entry to record this transaction on July 1, year 4.

On December 1, 2001, Graham Corporation incurs a 30-year, $300,000 mortgage liability upon purchase of a warehouse. This mortgage is payable in monthly installments of $3,086, which includes interest computed at the rate of 12% per year. The first monthly payment is made on December 31, 2001.

1   How much of the first payment made on December 31, 2001, is allocated to *repayment of principal*?

   $_____

2   What is the total liability related to this mortgage to be reported in Graham's balance sheet at December 31, 2001? (Do not separate into current and long-term portions.)

   $_____

3   The portion of the *second* monthly payment made on January 31, 2002, which represents *interest expense* is:

   $_____

4   What is the aggregate amount paid by Graham over the 30-year life of the mortgage?

   $_____

5   Over the 30-year life of the mortgage, the total amount Graham will pay for *interest charges* is:

   $_____

SOLUTIONS TO CHAPTER 10   10-MINUTE QUIZZES

QUIZ A		QUIZ B	
1	D	1	D
2	C	2	B
3	C	3	C
4	D	4	A
5	D	5	C

QUIZ C

1

Cash	10,200,000	
Bonds Payable...		10,000,000
Bond Interest Payable		200,000

Issued $10,000,000 face value bonds at par, plus two months' accrued interest.
($10,000,000 x 8% x 3/12 = $200,000)

2

Bond Interest Payable...	200,000	
Bond Interest Expense...	200,000	
Cash..		400,000

To record payment of semiannual interest. ($10,000,000 x 8% x 1/2)

3

$600,000 interest expense.

Since the bonds were issued at par, interest expense is equal to the contractual interest for the period that the bonds were outstanding. ($10,000,000 x 8% x 9/12 = $600,000)

4

$0 accrued bond interest payable.

The interest payment date is Dec. 31; therefore, interest for the last six months of a year is paid and does not appear as a liability in the balance sheet.

5

Bonds Payable	5,000,000	
Loss on Early Retirement of Bonds		
(Extraordinary Loss)	100,000	
Cash..		5,100,000

To record retirement of $5,000,000, face value bonds, originally issued at par, at 102.

© The McGraw-Hill Companies, Inc., 2003

Instructor's Resource Manual

QUIZ D

1

<u>**$86**</u> [$3,086 - $3,000 interest ($300,000 x .12 x 1/12)]

2

<u>**$299,914**</u> [$300,000 - $86 repayment of principal]

3

<u>**$2,999**</u> [$299,914 x .12 x 1/12 = $2,999]

4

<u>**$1,110,960**</u> [$3,086 monthly x 360 months]

5

<u>**$810,960**</u> [$1,110,960 total payments - $300,000 principal]

Assignment Guide to Chapter 10

	Exercises 1-15	Problems 1	2	3	4	5	6	7	Cases 1	2	3	4	Net 1
Time estimate (in minutes)	<15	40	40	25	30	30	30	60	25	25	30	30	25
Difficulty rating	E	M	M	S	M	M	M	S	E	M	M	M	M
Learning Objectives:													
1. Define *liabilities* and distinguish between current and long-term liabilities.	2, 3, 4	√	√					√	√				
2. Account for notes payable and interest expense.	2, 3	√	√	√									
3. Describe the costs relating to payrolls.	2, 5	√											
4. Prepare an amortization table allocating payments between interest and principal.	1, 2, 3, 6	√	√		√								
5. Describe corporate bonds and explain the tax advantage of debt financing.	2, 3, 4, 7, 8, 9, 10	√				√	√	√		√			√
6. Account for bonds issued at a discount or premium.	2, 3, 4, 9, 10	√					√	√		√			√
7. Explain the concept of present value as it relates to bond prices.										√			
8. Explain how estimated liabilities, loss contingencies, and commitments are disclosed in financial statements.	3, 4		√								√		
9. Evaluate the safety of creditors' claims.	11, 15							√	√	√			√
*10. Understand reporting issues related to leases, postretirement benefits, and deferred taxes.	12, 13, 14	√						√	√	√		√	

©The McGraw-Hill Companies, Inc., 2003
Instructor's Resource Manual

Chapter Summary

This, the first of two chapters on stockholders' equity, treats topics concerned with the paid-in capital of a corporation. Consideration of issues relative to retained earnings is deferred to Chapter 12.

The advantages and disadvantages of the corporate form are reviewed in detail, and the distinctions between public and closely held corporations are explained. An extensive discussion of the formation of a corporation highlights the rights of stockholders and the roles of corporate directors and officers.

The treatment of accounting procedures regarding paid-in capital concentrates on the issuance of capital stock and the stockholders' equity section of the balance sheet. The concept of par value is explained in detail, as is additional paid-in capital. The introduction of preferred stock leads to more complex illustrations of the stockholders' equity section. Preferences with respect to dividends and assets are explained and illustrated. Call and conversion features of preferred stock are also introduced. Other topics dealing with capital stock that are covered include issuance for assets other than cash, donated capital, and stock subscriptions.

The calculation of book value per common share is explained and illustrated before attention turns to factors concerning market values. The significance of market price to the issuing corporation is contrasted to its significance to the investor. We then explain the roles of interest rates and investor expectations in the determination of market prices.

Since stock splits and treasury stock transactions impact the presentation of paid-in capital on the balance sheet, they are also introduced in this chapter. Journal entries to record both the purchase and reissuance of treasury shares are provided. We explain and emphasize that profits and losses on treasury stock transactions are not recognized.

Learning Objectives

1. Discuss the advantages and disadvantages of organizing a business as a corporation.

2. Distinguish between publicly owned and closely held corporations.

3. Describe the rights of stockholders and the roles of corporate directors and officers.

4. Account for paid-in capital and prepare the equity section of a corporate balance sheet.

5. Contrast the features of common stock with those of preferred stock.

6. Discuss the factors affecting the market price of preferred and common stock.

7.   Explain the significance of par value, book value, and market value of capital stock.

8.   Explain the purpose and the effects of a stock split.

9.   Account for treasury stock transactions.

Brief topical outline

A Corporations – see *Case in Point* (page **463**)
  1 Why businesses incorporate – see *Your Turn* (page **463**)
  2 Publicly owned corporations – see *Case in Point* (page **464**)
    a Publicly owned corporations face different rules
B Formation of a corporation
  1 Organization costs
  2 Rights of stockholders
  3 Functions of the board of directors – see *Case in Point* (page **466**)
    a Functions of the corporate officers – see *Your Turn* (page **467**)
  4 Stockholder records in a corporation – see *Case in Point* (page **467**)
    a Stockholders subsidiary ledger
    b Stock transfer agent and stock registrar
C Paid-in capital of a corporation
  1 Authorization and issuance of capital stock
    a State laws affect the balance sheet presentation of stockholders' equity
    b Par value
    c Issuance of par value stock
    d No-par stock
  2 Common stocks and preferred stocks
  3 Characteristics of preferred stock
    a Stock preferred as to dividends – see *Case in Point* (page **471**)
    b Cumulative preferred stock
    c Stock preferred as to assets
    d Callable preferred stock
    e Convertible preferred stock
    f Other features of preferred stock – see *Management Strategy & Financial Reporting* (page **475**)
  4 Stock issued for assets other than cash
  5 Subscriptions to capital stock
  6 Donated capital – see *Case in Point* (page **475**)
  7 Book value per share of common stock
    a Book value when a company has both preferred and common stock - see *Cash Effects* (page **477**)
D Market value
  1 Accounting by the issuer
  2 Accounting by the investor – see *Case in Point* (page **477**)
  3 Market price of preferred stock - see *Case in Point* (page **478**)

      4   Market price of common stock - see *Your Turn* (page **479**)

      5   Book value and market price - see *Case in Point* (page **479**)

      6   Stock splits

      7   Treasury stock

      8   Recording purchases of treasury stock

          a   Treasury stock is not an asset

      9   Reissuance of treasury stock

          a   No profit or loss on treasury stock transactions

          b   Restrictions of retained earnings for treasury stock owned

      10   Stock buyback programs – see *Case in Point* and *Cash Effects* (page **483**)

    E Financial analysis – see *A Second Look* (page **485**)

Topical coverage and suggested assignment

Class Meetings on Chapter	Topical Outline Coverage	Homework Assignment (To Be Completed Prior to Class)				
		Discussion Questions	Exercises	Problems	Cases	Internet
1	A - B	1, 2, 4	1		3	1
2	C	5, 6, 7, 11	3, 4, 6	4, 5, 6		
3	D - E	15, 17, 18, 19	8, 9, 10	7, 8, 9	2	

Comments and observations

Teaching objectives for Chapter 11

In this chapter we provide a comprehensive introduction to factors affecting paid-in capital and its presentation on the balance sheet. Our teaching objectives are to:

1   Review the advantages and disadvantages of corporations.

2   Explain the nature of a publicly owned corporation.

3   Explain the roles of corporate directors and officers and the rights of stockholders.

4   Illustrate accounting for the issuance of capital stock in exchange for cash or other assets. Explain the role of an underwriter in the issuance of capital stock.

5   Discuss the typical features of *preferred* stock and contrast these features with those of *common* stock.

6   Explain when stock might be "subscribed".

7 Illustrate the computation of ***book value*** per share (with preferred stock outstanding). Distinguish among the concepts of ***book value, par value,*** and ***market value.***

8 Explain the most important determinants of the market values of preferred and common stock.

9 Explain the nature and purpose of ***stock splits.***

10 Explain the rationale for ***treasury stock*** transactions, and illustrate the related accounting entries.

New features in Chapter 11

In many respects this chapter parallels Chapter 11 of the previous edition. The organization of material has been changed to emphasize that this is a survey of topics related to paid-in capital. Coverage of proprietorships and partnerships has been eliminated. Issues affecting retained earnings have been treated in the chapter, which follows. Given that the theme is paid-in capital, stock-splits and treasury stock transactions have been moved to this chapter. New exercises and problems have been added to the end-of-chapter material to support this coverage. Additional new exercises and problems expand coverage of the stockholders' equity section of the balance sheet.

General comments

This chapter builds on the introduction to corporations earlier in the text. Because of the new terminology introduced, we always assign Exercise *2* and also advise students to study the list of key terms at the end of the chapter. We recommend assigning several exercises and problems requiring students to prepare the stockholders' equity section of a corporate balance sheet. The assignment material has been written to assist in this regard. Once students have a basic understanding of stockholders' equity, we find it helpful to review either Problem *5* or *6* in class, calling on students to explain their answers to each part. Exercise *5* is a shortened version of these problems and is suitable for use as a quiz.

In discussing preferred stock, we point out the similarities between preferred stock and long-term debt. You may find the asides below useful in such discussions.

We emphasize the relationship (or lack thereof) among par value, book value, and market value of a share of stock. Problem *7* is designed for this purpose and it can be covered quickly in class.

Discussion Question *16* makes the important point that secondary market activity does not directly affect the financial position of the company that issued the securities. We have been careful to make this point in the textbook and in our classrooms ever since the great stock market crash of 1987. This crash brought to our attention that even many senior accounting majors failed to recognize this point.

An aside The basic purpose of issuing preferred stock is to raise capital from a particular type of investor. Just as General Motors offers several makes of cars to attract different consumers, it offers several types of stock to appeal to different investors. In fact, GM now offers more "lines" of stock than of cars. The company produces five makes of automobile — Chevrolet, Pontiac, Buick, Oldsmobile, and Cadillac. However, it has outstanding eight issues of capital stock — five issues of preferred (three of which are convertible), its basic common stock, and two "special issues" of common stock (minority interests in several GM subsidiaries). Six of GM's eight stock issues are traded daily on the New York Stock Exchange; the other two are held by employee pension plans.

Another aside In some respects, preferred stock more closely resembles debt than equity. For example, preferred dividends are fixed in amount, rather than dependent upon the level of earnings. Also, preferred stockholders usually have no voting power. The key criterion distinguishing preferred stock from a liability is that liabilities mature — that is, they ultimately must be paid off. The SEC has taken the position that the *"redeemable"* preferred stock issued by several corporations should be classified in the balance sheet as debt rather than equity. The redeemable shares could be redeemed at their par value for cash, at the option of the shareholder. In making the decision, the SEC felt that the redemption option made the shares equivalent to demand notes payable rather than equity securities.

Supplemental Exercises

Business Week Exercise

In "Stocks: The Case for Unsplitting", *Business Week*, April 1, 2002, David Henry argues that companies which have lost share price as a result of *stock splits* should consider reverse *splits*. The articles discusses the potential benefits of reverse *splits*, including gaining the interest of institutional investors *and* the risk that reverse *splits* will cause frustrated investors to sell their *stock*. After reading the article, formulate a definition of a reverse stock split.

Group Exercise

Go to www.hp.com/financials/finhist/stock.hist.html and research the history of Hewlett-Packard's stock. Since going public how often has Hewlett-Packard split its common stock? What was the average share price prior to these splits? Discuss why the company split its shares on these occasions.

Internet Exercise

Access the 2001 annual report of Pepsico at http://www.pepsico.com/ and locate the consolidated balance sheet. How many shares of treasury stock does Pepsico own as of December 31, 2001?

Indicate the best answer for each question in the space provided.

_____ 1   Anders Corporation issued 150,000 shares of $5 par value capital stock at date of incorporation for cash at a price of $8 per share. During the first year of operations, the company earned $110,000 and declared a dividend of $75,000. At the end of this first year of operations, the balance of the Capital Stock account is:
   a $1,200,000.   c $750,000.
   b $1,310,000.   d $785,000.

_____ 2   Dryden Corporation has 100,000 shares of $1 par value common stock and 20,000 shares of 6% cumulative preferred stock, $100 par value, outstanding. The balance in Retained Earnings at the **beginning** of the year was $1,000,000, and one year's dividends were in arrears. Net income for the current year was $520,000. If Dryden Corporation paid a dividend of $2 per share on its common stock, what is the balance in Retained Earnings at the **end** of the year?
   a $1,320,000.   c $1,200,000.
   b $1,520,000.   d $1,080,000.

_____ 3   Eureka Corporation has total stockholders' equity of $8,800,000 as of December 31, 2001. The company has 300,000 shares of $2 par value common stock and 20,000 shares of 9% cumulative preferred stock, $100 par value, callable at a price of $110 per share, outstanding. Due to lower-than-expected net income, no dividends were declared by Eureka's board of directors for 2001. The **book value per share** of common stock is:
   a $22.00.   c $20.00.
   b $21.40.   d $22.67.

_____ 4   Which of the following most likely explains why a corporation's stock trades at a very high price-earnings ratio?
   a   Investors expect the corporation to have higher earnings in the future.
   b   The corporation pays a very low dividend on its stock.
   c   The corporation has several classes of stock outstanding.
   d   The corporation is large with very low risk.

_____ 5   Which of the following is **not** a characteristic of most preferred stocks?
   a   Preference as to dividends.
   b   No voting power.
   c   Convertible into common stock.
   d   Preference as to assets in the event of liquidation of the company.

Shown below is information relating to the stockholders' equity of Windrose Corporation at December 31, 2002:

8% cumulative preferred stock, $100 par, callable at $110, 50,000 shares authorized, 15,000 shares issued..	$1,500,000
Common stock, $5 par, 1,500,000 shares authorized, 1,200,000 shares issued and outstanding...	6,000,000
Additional paid-in capital: preferred stock	180,000
Additional paid-in capital: common stock...	4,800,000
Retained earnings	2,370,000

Answer the following questions based on the stockholders' equity section given above.

_____ 1 *Refer to the above data.* The *average issue price* per share of Windrose's *preferred* stock was:
   a $112.   b $100.   c $110.   d $56.

_____ 2 *Refer to the above data.* The total amount of Windrose's *paid-in capital* at December 31, 2002, is:
   a $7,500,000.
   b $2,370,000.
   c $12,480,000.
   d $4,980,000.

_____ 3 *Refer to the above data.* Windrose's total *legal capital* at December 31, 2002, is:
   a $12,480,000.
   b $10,500,000.
   c $9,870,000.
   d $7,500,000.

_____ 4 *Refer to the above data.* The *book value* per share of common stock, assuming current-year preferred dividends have been paid, is:
   a $9.00.   c $9.60.
   b $11.00.   d $12.38.

_____ 5 *Refer to the above data.* The balance in Retained Earnings at the beginning of the year was $1,950,000, and there were no dividends in arrears. Net income for 2002 was $2,940,000. What was the amount of dividend declared *on each share* of *common stock* during 2002?
   a $2.45.   c $2.00.
   b $2.08.   d $2.35.

CHAPTER 11   NAME_____ #_____

10-MINUTE QUIZ C   SECTION_____

Shown below is information relating to the stockholders' equity of Dartt Corporation at December 31, 2002:

8% cumulative preferred stock, $100 par, callable at $105, 100,000 shares authorized, 4,000 shares issued...	$ 400,000
Common stock, $2 par, 1,000,000 shares authorized, 500,000 shares issued and outstanding	1,000,000
Additional paid-in capital: preferred stock	100,000
Additional paid-in capital: common stock...	200,000
Retained earnings..	400,000

From the above information, compute the following:

1   The total amount of *legal capital*: $_____

2   The total amount of *paid-in capital*: $_____

3   The *average issue price* per share of *preferred* stock: $_____ per share

4   The *book value* per share of common stock (assume current-year preferred dividends have been paid) $_____ per share

5   The balance in Retained Earnings at the beginning of the year was $350,000, and there were no dividends in arrears. Net income for 2002 was $200,000. What was the amount of dividend declared *on each share* of *common stock* during 2002? $_____ per share

Shown below is the stockholders' equity section of Pilot Communication's balance sheet at *December 31, 2001*:

Stockholders' equity:
Common stock, $2 par value, 500,000 shares authorized,
　　?? shares issued... $ 600,000
Additional paid-in capital: common stock .... 　1,500,000
　　Total paid-in capital... $2,100,000
Retained earnings... 　1,800,000
Total stockholders' equity $3,900,000

In 2002, the following events occurred:

- Pilot Communication issued 2,000 shares of $2 par common stock as payment for legal services. Although Pilot's stock is not traded on any exchange, the agreed-upon value of the legal services is $60,000.

- Pilot Communication issued 6,000 shares of 6% cumulative preferred stock, $100 par value, for $108 per share.

- The board of directors declared a dividend of $1 per share on the common stock.

- Pilot's net income for 2002 was $600,000.

Instructions
Complete in good form the stockholders' equity section of a balance sheet prepared for Pilot Communication at *December 31, 2002*:

Stockholders' equity:	
6% cumulative preferred stock, $100 par value,	
10,000 shares authorized, 6,000 shares issued	$
Total paid-in capital	$
Retained earnings	$
Total stockholders' equity	$

SOLUTIONS TO CHAPTER 11   10-MINUTE QUIZZES

QUIZ A		QUIZ B	
1	C	1	A
2	D	2	C
3	B	3	D
4	A	4	B
5	C	5	C

QUIZ C

1

$400,000 + $1,000,000 = $1,400,000 total legal capital

2

$400,000 + $1,000,000 + $100,000 + $200,000 = $1,700,000 total paid-in capital

3

($400,000 + $100,000)/4,000 shares = $125 per share

4

$400,000 + $1,000,000 + $100,000 + $200,000 + $400,000 = $2,100,000 total stockholders' equity

$2,100,000 - $420,000 (call price of preferred) = $1,680,000

$1,680,000 stockholders' equity allocable to common stock/500,000 shares common stock outstanding = $3.36 book value per share of common stock

5

Retained earnings, beginning of year	$350,000
Net income	200,000
Subtotal	$550,000
Less: Retained earnings, end of year	(400,000)
Retained earnings declared as dividends	$150,000
Less: Dividends on preferred stock	(32,000)
Amount of dividends to common stockholders	$118,000

$118,000/500,000 shares common stock = $.236 dividend per share

QUIZ D

Stockholders' equity:

6% cumulative preferred stock, $100 par value, 10,000 shares authorized, 6,000 shares issued	$ 600,000
Common stock, $2 par value, 500,000 shares authorized, 302,000 shares issued	604,000
Additional paid-in capital: Preferred	48,000
Additional paid-in capital: Common	1,556,000
Total paid-in capital	$2,808,000
Retained earnings	2,062,000*
Total stockholders' equity	$4,870,000

*Computation

Beginning retained earnings	$1,800,000
Add: Net income for 2002	600,000
Less: Dividends declared ($302,000 common + $36,000 preferred)	(338,000)
Retained earnings, Dec. 31, 2002	$2,062,000

Assignment Guide to Chapter 11

	Exercises	Problems									Cases				Net
	1-13	1	2	3	4	5	6	7	8	9	1	2	3	4	1
Time estimate (in minutes)	<15	40	40	25	30	60	25	25	25	30	30	25	40	40	25
Difficulty rating	E	M	M	S	M	S	E	M	Na	M	M	M	E	M	M
Learning Objectives:															
1. Discuss the advantages and disadvantages of organizing a business as a corporation.	1, 2														
2. Distinguish between publicly owned and closely held corporations.	1, 2, 6						√						√		
3. Describe the rights of stockholders and the roles of corporate directors and officers.	1, 2						√						√		
4. Account for paid-in capital and prepare the equity section of a corporate balance sheet.	2, 3, 4, 5, 6, 7, 8, 12, 13	√	√	√	√	√	√	√	√	√					√
5. Contrast the features of common stock with those of preferred stock.	2, 3, 4, 5, 8	√	√	√	√	√	√	√	√	√					√
6. Discuss the factors affecting the market price of preferred stock and common stock.	2, 5, 8	√	√	√			√							√	
7. Explain the significance of par value, book value, and market value of capital stock.	2, 5, 7, 8, 13	√					√	√	√	√		√			√
8. Explain the purpose and effects of a stock split.	2, 10									√					
9. Account for treasury stock transactions.	2, 9, 11								√	√					√

Chapter Summary

Chapter 12 continues the coverage of stockholders' equity but shifts the focus from paid-in capital to retained earnings. The student is already aware that net income drives the changes in retained earnings. However, in any given period net income may reflect unusual and nonrecurring events. We begin by explaining how to define such items and how to present them so that the income statement may still serve as the basis for reasonable estimates of future earnings. The three categories of events, which require special treatment, are (1) discontinued operations, (2) extraordinary items, and (3) changes in accounting principle. Each item is explained and illustrated with a Case in Point capsule based on the experience of an actual company.

Before turning to the impact of various dividend transactions, we briefly review basic and diluted earnings per share. The emphasis here is on interpretation of the EPS figures, since the detailed mechanics of calculating these measures is beyond the scope of the first course.

The second major section of the chapter explains a number of stockholder equity transactions that affect retained earnings. The most obvious example of such transactions is the declaration of a cash dividend. The requirements for distributing a cash dividend are outlined as are the significant dates involved in the distribution of the dividend. Stock dividends are discussed since they too result in a reduction in retained earnings. This portion of the chapter closes with a brief explanation of prior period adjustments to retained earnings.

Additional topics covered in Chapter 12 include an introduction to comprehensive income and a review of the statement of stockholders' equity.

Learning Objectives

1.   Describe how discontinued operations, extraordinary items, and accounting changes are presented in the income statement.

2.   Compute earnings per share.

3.   Distinguish between basic and diluted earnings per share.

4.   Account for cash dividends and stock dividends, and explain the effects of these transactions on a company's financial statements.

5.   Describe and prepare a statement of retained earnings.

6.   Define ***prior period adjustments***, and explain how they are presented in financial statements.

7. Define *comprehensive income*, and explain how it differs from net income.

8. Describe and prepare a statement of stockholders' equity.

Brief topical outline

A Reporting the results of operations
  1 Developing predictive information – see *Management Strategy & Financial Reporting* (page **505**)
  2 Reporting irregular items: an illustration
  3 Continuing operations
    a Income from continuing operations
  4 Discontinued operations
    a Discontinued operations are not really unusual – see *Case in Point* (page **506**)
  5 Extraordinary items
    a Other unusual gains and losses – see *Case in Point* (page **507**)
    b Distinguishing between the unusual and the extraordinary – see *Case in Point* (page **508**)
    c Restructuring charges – see *Case in Point* (page **508**)
  6 Changes in accounting principle
    a The cumulative effect of an accounting change
    b Changes in principle versus changes in estimate – see *Your Turn* (page **509**)
  7 Earnings per share (EPS)
    a Computing earnings per share
    b What happens if more shares are issued?
    c Preferred dividends and earnings per share
    d Presentation of earnings per share in the income statement
    e Interpreting the different per-share amounts
B Financial analysis – see *Case in Point* (page **512**)
  1 Basic and diluted earnings per share – see *Management Strategy & Financial Reporting* (page **513**)
C Other transactions affecting retained earnings
  1 Cash dividends – see *Your Turn* (page **514**)
  2 Dividend dates
  3 Liquidating dividends
  4 Stock dividends
    a Entries to record a stock dividend
    b Reasons for stock dividends – see *Case in Point* (page **517**)
    c Distinctions between stock splits and stock dividends
  5 Statement of retained earnings
  6 Prior period adjustments
    a Restrictions of retained earnings
  7 Comprehensive income – see *Cash Effects* (page **520**)

8   Statement of stockholders' equity

9   Stockholders' equity section of the balance sheet – see *A Second Look* (page **522**)

Topical coverage and suggested assignment

Class Meetings on Chapter	Topical Outline Coverage	Homework Assignment (To Be Completed Prior to Class)				
		Discussion Questions	Exercises	Problems	Cases	Internet
1	A	1, 2, 3, 5	1, 3, 4, 5	1, 3	3, 6	1
2	B - C	9, 10, 14, 16, 18	7, 8, 10, 11	4, 6, 7	4	

Comments and observations

Teaching objectives for Chapter 12

In this chapter, we discuss a variety of events and transactions that affect retained earnings. In the classroom, our objectives are to:

1   Explain the purpose of reporting irregular events separately from normal and recurring business activities.

2   Carefully define *discontinued operations, extraordinary items*, and *accounting changes.* Review and discuss the financial statement presentation of each category of event.

3   Illustrate the computation of *earnings per share*, and briefly discuss the distinction between *basic* and *diluted* earnings.

4   Discuss the nature and purpose of *cash dividends* and *stock dividends*, emphasizing the effects upon total stockholders' equity and the probable effects upon stock price. Illustrate the journal entries for each of the events.

5   Explain the nature of *prior period adjustments.* Discuss probability of occurrence in publicly owned and closely held corporations.

6   Review and discuss the *statement of retained earnings.*

7   Explain the nature of comprehensive income.

8   Review the *statement of stockholders' equity* portrayed as an "expanded" statement of retained earnings.

New features in Chapter 12

The changes to this chapter reflect the new organization of the material on stockholders' equity. We have moved the prior treatments of stock splits and treasury stock transactions to Chapter 11 so that we might concentrate on retained earnings. In most other respects, the coverage of topics in this chapter parallels that in our previous edition. A section discussing the concept of comprehensive income has been added. The *Case in Point* capsules have all been updated. The assignment material has been expanded to include an exercise on comprehensive income.

General comments

Many accounting faculty ask us why we cover discontinued operations in the introductory course. Our answer is that in this era of "corporate restructuring," discontinued operations are commonplace in the financial statements of publicly owned corporations. Discontinued operations are far more commonplace (and more material in dollar amount) than are extraordinary items. (Prior period adjustments, by comparison, are virtually nonexistent in the financial statements of large corporations.)

We make these points in the text but feel that we owe a separate explanation to instructors. While extraordinary items and prior period adjustments are "traditional" accounting topics, discontinued operations is a relative newcomer. We also know that some introductory accounting textbooks still do not address this emerging topic.

In discussing irregular events, we focus upon the appropriate financial statement presentation rather than upon the recording of transactions. Most of these transactions are recorded in the same manner as ordinary transactions. Allocations of revenue, expenses, and gains and losses to such special categories as "continuing operations," "discontinued operations," and "extraordinary items" are made on a working paper at the end of the period. The tax effects relating to these items also are determined and allocated on a working paper rather than through journal entries.

We consider these working paper procedures beyond the scope of the introductory course. Entries to record accounting changes and prior period adjustments also are beyond the scope of the introductory accounting course. Anyone with responsibility for recording such transactions needs more of an accounting background than an introductory course can provide. Any user of financial statements, however, needs to understand the nature of these unusual items in order to interpret properly the operating results of the current period.

Several of our problems are intended to illustrate the presentation of irregular events in financial statements, including Problems *1, 2,* and *3*. These problems are successively comprehensive and challenging. We also recommend class discussion of Case *1* involving several well-known corporations.

In discussing earnings-per-share, we consider a conceptual understanding important, but regard most of the mechanics of per-share computations as beyond the scope of the course. For instance, we discuss the concept of diluted earnings-per-share, but do not get into any computations. We do, however, review Exercise *5*. This exercise helps clarify the idea that earnings-per-share is based only upon the income applicable to common stock.

The "stockholders' equity" portion of this chapter includes a variety of short topics. We find an in-class review of Exercises *8, 9*, and *10* is an efficient way to cover many of these topics. As an overview, we use Problem *5*, which also acquaints students with the unofficial "statement" of stockholders' equity.

Supplemental Exercises

Business Week Exercise

The article "What's an Old-Line CEO To Do?", *Business Week,* March 27, 2000, lists the ten companies which experienced the greatest increases in the market value of their equity, and the ten which experienced the greatest decreases. Research these companies in "Fourth-Quarter and Full Year 1999 Corporate Scorecard", *Business Week,* February 28, 2000. How do the winners and losers compare in terms of EPS?

Group Exercise

The text points out that restructuring charges have been very common during the 1990's. Visit websites for several large corporations, find the 2001 annual reports and study the notes to the financial statements for information on restructuring charges incurred by the corporations.

Internet Exercise

Visit websites for several large corporations, find the 2001 annual reports and review the income statements. Report on discontinued operations and extraordinary items.

Indicate the best answer for each question in the space provided.

_____　**1**　Apex Corporation declared a 2-for-1 common stock split, but this transaction was erroneously recorded as a 100% common stock dividend. As a result:

　　a　The common stock account is overstated.

　　b　The total dollar amount of stockholders' equity is overstated.

　　c　The corporate records do not show the correct number of shares of common stock outstanding.

　　d　The par value per share is understated.

_____　**2**　Courtney Mfg.'s financial statements for the current year include the following:

Income from continuing operations..	$728,000
Prior-period adjustment (increase in prior-year net income, net of taxes)..	126,000
Cash dividends paid to preferred stockholders...	145,000
Gain from discontinued operations (net of taxes)..	434,000
Cumulative effect of accounting change (reduction in net income, net of tax benefit)	308,000
Extraordinary loss (net of tax benefit)	119,000

　　On the basis of this information, net income for the current year is:

　　a　$590,000.　　**b**　$716,000.　　**c**　$680,000.　　**d**　$735,000.

_____　**3**　The following two items are disclosed in the stockholders' equity section of Clark Corporation's December 31, 2001, balance sheet:

Treasury stock (500 shares, at cost)...	$15,000
Additional paid-in capital: treasury stock transactions..............................	5,000

　　If the company had reacquired 3,000 shares of treasury stock in February of 2001, then some of the treasury stock must have been sold during 2001 for:

　　a　$2 per share above its par value.　　**c**　$32 per share.

　　b　$2 per share.　　　　　　　　　　**d**　$32 per share above its cost.

_____　**4**　At the beginning of the current year, Kersey Corporation had 400,000 shares of $1 par common stock outstanding and had retained earnings of $7,000,000. During the year, the company earned $5,000,000, declared a 5% stock dividend when the price of stock was $25 per share, and paid a year-end cash dividend of $2 per share. (The cash dividend was paid after the stock dividend had been distributed.) Kersey Corporation's retained earnings at the *end* of the year amount to:

　　a　$12,000,000.　　**b**　$10,660,000.　　**c**　$11,140,000.　　**d**　$11,160,000.

_____　**5**　Nesbit Corp. had 25,000 shares of 8% preferred stock, $100 par, and 250,000 shares of $1 par common stock outstanding throughout the year. Net income for the year was $1,100,000, and Nesbit declared and distributed a cash dividend of $2 per share on its common stock. Earnings per share amounted to:

　　a　$4.40.　　**b**　$2.00.　　**c**　$3.60.　　**d**　$1.60.

10-MINUTE QUIZ B   SECTION_____

The stockholders' equity section of the balance sheet of Hansen Publishing at December 31, 2001, appears as follows:

Stockholders' equity:

5% preferred stock, $100 par, callable at $115,	
50,000 shares authorized, ?? shares issued...	$1,600,000
Common stock, $2 par, 500,000 shares authorized,	
120,000 shares issued, of which ?? are held in treasury.......................................	240,000
Additional paid-in capital:	
From issuance of preferred stock...	160,000
From issuance of common stock...	600,000
From treasury stock transactions..	6,000
From common stock dividends..	100,000
Total paid-in capital	$2,706,000
Retained earnings ($96,000 equal to cost of treasury	
stock is not available for dividends)	680,000
	$3,386,000
Less: Treasury stock (at cost: 12,000 common shares)...	(96,000)
Total stockholders' equity...	$3,290,000

Answer the following questions based on the stockholders' equity section given above.

_____ 1 ***Refer to the above data.*** What was the average issue price per share of ***preferred stock?***

   a $88.   b $100.   c $110.   d $108.

_____ 2 ***Refer to the above data.*** How many shares of ***common stock*** are outstanding?

   a   120,000.   b   108,000.   c   500,000.   d   96,000.

_____ 3 ***Refer to the above data.*** A small stock dividend of 5,000 shares was declared and distributed during 2001. What was the market price per share on the date of declaration?

   a $22 per share.   b $20 per share.   c $2 per share.   d $18 per share.

_____ 4 ***Refer to the above data.*** If Hansen Publishing had reacquired 14,000 shares of treasury stock early in 2001, then some treasury stock must have been sold during 2001 for:

   a $5 per share.   b $8 per share.   c $3 per share.   d $11 per share.

_____ 5 ***Refer to the above data.*** Assume that all remaining treasury stock is reissued at a price of $13 per share in January of 2002. What amount should be credited to the account Additional Paid-in Capital: Treasury Stock Transactions in the journal entry to record this transaction?

   a $96,000.   b $60,000.   c $156,000.   d $66,000.

The stockholders' equity section of the balance sheet of Papillon Fashions, Inc., at December 31, 2001, appears as follows:

Stockholders' equity:
7% preferred stock, $100 par, callable at $105, 50,000 shares authorized, 40,000 shares issued	$4,000,000
Common stock, $2 par, 500,000 shares authorized, 300,000 shares issued, of which 30,000 are held in treasury	600,000
Additional paid-in capital:	
From issuance of preferred stock...	480,000
From issuance of common stock...	1,410,000
From treasury stock transactions...	25,000
From common stock dividends..	250,000
Total paid-in capital	$6,765,000
Retained earnings ($240,000 equal to cost of treasury stock is not available for dividends)	1,700,000
	$8,465,000
Less: Treasury stock (at cost: 30,000 common shares)	(240,000)
Total stockholders' equity...	$8,225,000

Answer the following questions based on the stockholders' equity section given above.

1   *Refer to the above data.* What was the average issue price per share of *preferred stock*?
$_____ per share

2   *Refer to the above data.* How many shares of *common stock* are outstanding? _____ shares

3   *Refer to the above data.* A small stock dividend of 20,000 shares was declared and distributed during 2001. What was the market price per share on the date of declaration?
$_____ per share

4   *Refer to the above data.* If Papillon Fashions had reacquired 35,000 shares of treasury stock early in 2001, compute the price per share for which the reissued treasury stock was sold. $_____ per share

5   *Refer to the above data.* Assume all remaining treasury stock is reissued at a price of $15 per share in January of 2002. Give the journal entry to record this transaction:

Shown below is information relating to operations of Mary Tech. for the current year:

Continuing operations:
Net sales.. $5,000,000
Costs and expenses (including income taxes).. 4,000,000
Other data:
Current-year loss generated by segment of the business
  discontinued in July (net of income benefit)... 400,000
Gain on disposal of discontinued segment (net of
  income tax).. 250,000
Prior-period adjustment (decrease in prior years' depreciation
  expense, net of income taxes)... 100,000
Cumulative effect of change in accounting principle
  (increase in net income, net of related income tax)..................................... 300,000
Extraordinary loss (net of income tax benefit)... 40,000
Cash dividends declared ($2 per share) 200,000

In the space provided, complete the income statement for Mary Tech., including earnings per share figures. Mary Tech. has 100,000 shares of a single class of common stock outstanding throughout the year.

MARY TECH.
Condensed Income Statement
For the Year Ended December 31, 2001

Net sales .... $

Earnings per share:

SOLUTIONS TO CHAPTER 12   10-MINUTE QUIZZES

QUIZ A
1   A
2   D
3   C
4   B
5   C

QUIZ B
1   C
2   B
3   A
4   D
5   B

QUIZ C

1

Average issue price per share of preferred stock: $112 per share
($4,000,000 + $480,000)/40,000 shares = $112 per share

2

270,000 shares of common stock outstanding: 300,000 shares issued - 30,000 held in treasury = 270,000 shares

3

Market price per share on stock dividend declaration date: $14.50

$250,000/20,000 shares = $12.50 market value in excess of par
$2 par value + $12.50 excess over par (above) = $14.50 per share

4

5,000 shares of treasury stock reissued at $13 per share

5,000 shares treasury stock reissued (35,000 - 30,000 remaining)
$25,000/5,000 shares = $5 per share *in excess of cost* was received when the shares were reissued.
$240,000/30,000 shares left = $8 cost + $5 (above) = $13 reissue price

5

Cash (30,000 shares x $15 per share)	450,000	
Treasury Stock		240,000
Additional Paid-In Capital: Treasury		
Stock Transactions...		210,000

Instructor's Resource Manual

QUIZ D

MARY TECH.
Condensed Income Statement
For the Year Ended December 31, 2001

Net sales		$ 5,000,000
Cost and expenses (including applicable		
income taxes)		(4,000,000)
Income from continuing operations...................................		$ 1,000,000
Discontinued operations:		
Operating loss (net of income tax benefits)	$(400,000)	
Gain on disposal (net of income taxes).........................	250,000	(150,000)
Income before extraordinary items and cumulative		
effect of accounting change		$850,000
Extraordinary loss (net of income tax benefit)	$(40,000)	
Cumulative effect of accounting change		
(net of income tax benefit)..	300,000	260,000
Net income...		$1,110,000
Earnings per share:		
Earnings from continuing operations		
($1,000,000 ÷ 100,000 shares).......................................		$ 10.00
Loss from discontinued operations		
($150,000 ÷ 100,000 shares)		(1.50)
Earnings before extraordinary item and cumulative effect		
of accounting change ($1,500,000 ÷ 100,000 shares).....................		$ 8.50
Extraordinary loss ($40,000 ÷ 100,000 shares).......................................		(.40)
Cumulative effect of accounting change		
($300,000 ÷ 100,000 shares)...		3.00
Net earnings ($1,110,000 ÷ 100,000 shares)		$11.10

Assignment Guide to Chapter 12

Learning Objectives:	Exercises	Problems									Cases						Net
	1–13	1	2	3	4	5	6	7	8	9	1	2	3	4	5	6	1
Time estimate (in minutes)	<15	40	40	25	30	60	25	25	25	30	30	25	40	40	25	40	40
Difficulty rating	E	M	M	S	M	S	E	M	M	M	M	M	E	M	M	E	M
1. Describe how discontinued operations, extraordinary items, and accounting changes are presented in the income statement.	2, 3, 4, 11, 13	√	√													√	
2. Compute earnings per share.	2, 3, 4, 5, 6, 10	√	√	√						√	√	√	√		√	√	
3. Distinguish between basic and diluted earnings per share.	2			√						√	√		√		√		√
4. Account for cash dividends and stock dividends, and explain the effects of these transactions on a company's financial statements.	1, 2, 6, 7, 8, 10				√	√	√		√				√				
5. Describe and prepare a statement of retained earnings.	11																
6. Define *prior period adjustments*, and explain how they are presented in financial statements.	2																
7. Define *comprehensive income*, and explain how it differs from net income.	2, 12							√									
8. Describe and prepare a statement of stockholders' equity.	9, 11, 13					√		√						√			

©The McGraw-Hill Companies, Inc., 2003
Instructor's Resource Manual

Chapter Summary

The statement of cash flows was introduced in Chapter 1. This chapter begins by reviewing the purpose of the statement. Its usefulness to creditors and investors in evaluating solvency is emphasized from the outset. The classification of cash transactions into operating, investing, and financing activities is explained in full. This section includes an explanation of the reasoning behind the classification of interest receipts, interest payments, and dividend receipts as operating activities. We also take the opportunity at the outset to highlight the importance of cash flows from operating activities.

The approach to preparing the statement centers on analyzing the income statement and the associated changes in noncash balance sheet accounts. The approach is introduced using a simple illustration based on changes in the balance of the marketable securities account. We then apply this methodology to an example that develops the entire statement.

The direct method is used to compute cash flows from operating activities. Discussion of the indirect method is also presented. Either or both methods may be chosen at the option of the instructor. Using a worksheet for preparing the statement of cash flows is presented as a *Supplemental Topic*.

The analysis of flows from investing and financing activities is somewhat simpler than that for operating activities and the coverage is as a result relatively brief.

The chapter concludes with a detailed discussion of the use of the SCF in developing strategies to manage cash flows. Emphasis here is on the use of the accounting information by internal management rather than investors and creditors external to the firm.

Learning Objectives

1. Explain the purposes and uses of a statement of cash flows.

2. Describe how cash transactions are classified in a statement of cash flows.

3. Compute the major cash flows relating to operating activities.

4. Compute the cash flows relating to investing and financing activities.

5. Distinguish between the direct and indirect methods of reporting operating cash flows.

6. Explain why net income differs from net cash flow from operating activities.

7. Compute net cash flows from operating activities using the *indirect method*.

8. Discuss the likely effects of various business strategies on cash flows.

*9. Explain how a worksheet may be helpful in preparing a statement of cash flows.

Brief topical outline

A Statement of cash flows
  1 Purposes of the statement - see *Case in Point* (page **544**)
  2 Example of a statement of cash flows
    a Classification of cash flows
    b Operating activities
    c Investing activities
    d Financing activities
    e Why are receipts and payments of interest classified as operating activities
    f Cash and cash equivalents - see *Case in Point* (page **547**)
  3 The approach to preparing a statement of cash flows
B Preparing a statement of cash flows: an illustration
  1 Operating activities
  2 Investing activities
  3 Financing activities
  4 Cash and cash equivalents
  5 Cash flows from operating activities
    a Cash received from customers
    b Interest and dividends received
  6 Cash payments for merchandise and for expenses
    a Cash paid for purchases of merchandise – see *Management Strategy and Financial Reporting* (page **553**)
    b Cash payments for expenses
    c Cash paid to suppliers and employees
    d Cash payments for interest and taxes
    e A quick review – see *Case in Point* (page **555**)
  7 Cash flows from investing activities
    a Purchases and sales of securities
    b Loans made and collected – see *Your Turn* (page **556**)
    c Cash paid to acquire plant assets
    d Proceeds from sales of plant assets
    e A quick review
  8 Cash flows from financing activities
    a Short-term borrowing transactions
    b Proceeds from issuing bonds payable and capital stock

Topical coverage and suggested assignment

Class Meetings on Chapter	Topical Outline Coverage	Homework Assignment (To Be Completed Prior to Class)				
		Discussion Questions	Exercises	Problems	Cases	Internet
1	A	1, 2, 4, 6	1, 2	1	1	
2	B	6, 9, 10, 13	3, 4, 5, 6, 7	2, 3, 4		1
3	C-*F	18, 20, 23, 24	8, *9, *10	6, 7, *8	2, 4	

*Optional assignment, time permitting.

Comments and observations

Teaching objectives for Chapter 13

In presenting the statement of cash flows, our teaching objectives are to:

1   Explain the content and usefulness of this financial statement.

2   Provide a brief history of this financial statement, distinguishing it from the statement of changes in financial position and emphasizing the need for information regarding cash flows in this era of corporate "takeovers."

3   Describe the major classifications within the statement of cash flows. Emphasize the relative importance of the net cash flow from operating activities.

4   Briefly explain why it is that accounting records maintained on the accrual basis of accounting do not show cash flows as balances of specific ledger accounts.

5   Explain how cash flows may be determined by examining income statement accounts and the changes in related balance sheet accounts. [Illustrate with such accounts as Marketable Securities and Gain (or Loss) on Marketable Securities.]

6   Illustrate the computation of the basic cash flows (direct method) relating to operating activities. Emphasize the rationale underlying each computation.

7   Explain the basic reasons why net cash flow from operating activities may differ from the amount of net income.

8   Illustrate the computation of cash flows relating to investing and financing activities. Again, emphasize the rationale underlying each computation.

9   Briefly compare and contrast the direct and indirect methods of reporting net cash flows from operating activities.

10 Discuss the critical importance of managing cash flows and introduce strategic options for management to improve cash flows from existing operations.

New features in Chapter 13
In most respects our coverage in this chapter is identical to that in our preceding edition. *Case in Point* capsules have been updated and we have added *Management Strategy* capsules.

General comments

When the FASB acted to replace the statement of changes in financial position with a new financial statement—a statement of cash flows—we believe the Board significantly improved the quality of financial reporting and accounting education. The old statement of financial position was difficult to read, to understand, and to teach. It could be prepared on any of several bases—including cash, working capital, and net quick assets. The "funds statements" included in the annual reports of major companies were difficult to interpret and seldom comparable, and they usually bore little resemblance to the textbook illustrations. And teaching "funds flow" was not easy, especially at the introductory level. Typical teaching approaches usually involved complicated working papers, mythical T accounts, and numerous confusing adjustments to the net income figure.

We find the new statement of cash flows intuitively logical. Therefore, it should be more meaningful to readers of financial statements and easier to explain in the classroom. The phenomenon of cash flows from operations is now explained by such easy-to-understand captions as "Cash collected from customers" and "Cash paid to suppliers and employees." Compare this to the old approach of "Net income, plus depreciation, minus nonoperative gains, plus nonoperative losses, etc., etc."

The direct and indirect methods One area of controversy in presenting cash flows is whether to use the *direct* or *indirect* method of determining the cash flow from operating activities. The FASB recommends use of the direct method, but at present, the indirect method is far more widely used in practice.

Without question, we opt for the *direct method.* Introductory students are able to *understand* the direct method, as it explains in straightforward terms the nature of the cash flows comprising "operating activities." The indirect method is an abstraction, meaningful only to someone who already understands clearly the differences between the accrual and cash bases of accounting. Thus, we consider the direct method a "gift from heaven" to the introductory accounting instructor.

Of course, not everyone sees it our way. Therefore we also present the *indirect* approach. A *Supplemental Topic* presents a worksheet approach to the indirect method.

Supplemental Exercises

Business Week Exercise

In "NexMed: Unbowed Despite CPA Doubts", *Business Week*, April 15, 2001, Gene Marcial evaluates NexMed, a biotechnology company. PricewaterhouseCoopers expressed "substantial doubt" about the biotech's viability as a going concern, citing recurring losses and negative *cash flows* from operations. After reading the article, write a 1-2 paragraph essay on how negative cash flows can affect an external auditor's opinion on the future of a company.

Group Exercise

The text states that the primary tool used by management to anticipate and shape future cash flows is a cash budget. Read "Not-so-Liquid Assets", *Business Week Online*, September 27, 2001, to see what small business owners say about their worst problem: coping with cash flow troubles while trying to collect. How does this article relate to what you have studied about cash flows in chapter 13?

Internet Exercise

Obtain the 2001 Annual Report for MCIWorldCom at www.mciworldcom.com. Examine the balance sheet. What amount of current liabilities is the company reporting as of the end of 2001? Now obtain the statement of cash flows. How much cash did MCIWorldCom generate from operating activities during 2001? Was this net cash flow from operating activities sufficient to pay the company's current liabilities? If not, how did the company obtain the necessary cash to remain solvent?

Using the above information, indicate the best answer for each question in the space provided.

In order to prepare the statement of cash flows for Tinker Toys Corporation for 2001, the accountant has compiled the following data regarding cash flows:

Cash paid to acquire marketable securities...	$ 390,000
Proceeds from sale of marketable securities...	37,500
Proceeds from issuance of capital stock..	300,000
Proceeds from issuance of bonds payable...	75,000
Payments to settle short-term debt..	52,500
Interest and dividends received...	30,000
Cash received from customers..	?
Dividends paid	150,000
Cash paid to suppliers and employees..	1,050,000
Interest paid	45,000
Income taxes paid...	90,000
Cash and cash equivalents, January 1, 2001..	63,000
Cash and cash equivalents, December 31, 2001...	78,000

_____ 1   Tinker Toys' cash flow from *investing activities* during 2001 is:
      a $390,000 net cash used by investing activities.
      b $322,500 net cash provided by investing activities.
      c $352,500 net cash used by investing activities.
      d $360,000 net cash used by investing activities.

_____ 2   Tinker Toys' cash flow from *financing activities* during 2001 is:
      a $322,500 net cash provided by financing activities.
      b $172,500 net cash provided by financing activities.
      c $127,500 net cash provided by financing activities.
      d $375,000 net cash provided by financing activities.

_____ 3   Tinker Toys' cash flow from *operating activities* during 2001 is:
      a $45,000 net cash provided by operating activities.
      b $1,155,000 net cash used by operating activities.
      c $240,000 net cash provided by operating activities.
      d $195,000 net cash provided by operating activities.

_____ 4   In the 2001 statement of cash flows for Tinker Toys Corporation, the amount of *cash received from customers* is:
      a $1,350,000.
      b $1,395,000.
      c $1,200,000.
      d $1,380,000.

Use the following information for questions 1 through 4.

Totally Corporation's statement of cash flows for 2001 shows the following *investing activities*:

Proceeds from sale of marketable securities..	$ 110,000
Purchase of land..	(190,000)
Proceeds from sale of land..	90,000
Net cash provided by investing activities	$ 10,000

Totally's income statement for 2001 includes the following:

Loss on sale of marketable securities...	$12,000
Gain on disposal of land	20,000

_____   1   *Refer to the above data.* The *cost* of the land sold during 2001 was:
              a $80,000.   b $90,000.   c $110,000.   d $70,000.

_____   2   *Refer to the above data.* The *cost* (*book value*) of the marketable securities sold
              during 2001 was:
              a $122,000.   c $110,000
              b $98,000.   d   Some other amount.

_____   3   *Refer to the above data.* Totally's balance sheet at the end of 2000
              showed Land of $100,000. On the basis of the data presented above, compute the
              amount to be reported for Land in Totally Corporation's balance sheet at
              December 31, 2001.
              a $200,000.   c $220,000
              b $320,000.   d   Some other amount.

_____   4   *Refer to the above data.* Totally's balance sheet at the end of 2000 showed
              Investment in Marketable Securities at $250,000. On the basis of the data
              presented above, compute the amount to be reported for Investment in Marketable
              Securities in Totally Corporation's balance sheet at *December 31, 2001.*
              a $128,000.   b $372,000.   c $360,000.   d $140,000.

_____   5   Which of the following correctly describes a difference between the *direct*
              method and the *indirect* method of computing operating cash flow?
              a   The direct method is used when accounting records are kept on a cash basis;
                  the indirect method is used when accounting records are maintained on an
                  accrual basis.
              b   The direct method may be used only when a company maintains special
                  journals for cash receipts and cash disbursements; the indirect method is used
                  in all other situations.
              c   Both the direct and the indirect methods result in the same net cash flow
                  from operating activities, but the format of this section of the statement of
                  cash flows is different under the alternative methods.
              d   The direct method is used when all accounting records and bank statements
                  are available; the indirect method is used when some accounting records or
                  documents are missing or have been destroyed.

Using the following information, complete the statement of cash flows for Mandarin Foods for the year ended December 31, 2001. Place parentheses around those figures in the statement representing cash outlays.

Payments for purchase of land	$ 520,000
Proceeds from sale of land	50,000
Proceeds from issuance of capital stock	400,000
Proceeds from issuance of bonds payable	100,000
Payments to settle short-term debt	70,000
Interest and dividends received	40,000
Cash received from customers	1,800,000
Dividends paid	200,000
Cash paid to suppliers and employees	1,400,000
Interest paid	60,000
Income taxes paid	120,000
Cash and cash equivalents, January 1, 2001	84,000
Cash and cash equivalents, December 31, 2001	?

MANDARIN FOODS
Statement of Cash Flows
For the Year Ended December 31, 2001

Cash flows from operating activities (direct method):
    Cash received from customers.. $ _____

    Cash provided by operating activities...................................... $ _____
           $ _____

    Cash disbursed for operating activities .... _____ (_____)
       Net cash flow from operating activities................................. $ _____
Cash flow from investing activities:
           $ _____

       Net cash used by investing activities...................................... _____ (_____)
Cash flows from financing activities:
           $ _____

       Net cash provided by financing activities .... _____
Net increase (decrease) in cash.. $ _____

Cash and cash equivalents, beginning of year .... _____

Cash and cash equivalents, end of year .... $ _____

10-MINUTE QUIZ D   SECTION_____

The following *balance sheets* are provided for Seaview Dairy:

	End of Year	Beginning of Year
Cash and cash equivalents...	$140,000	$110,000
Accounts receivable	50,000	55,000
Inventory	110,000	140,000
Plant and equipment (net)..	100,000	70,000
Total assets	$400,000	$375,000
Accounts payable..	$ 35,000	$ 25,000
Wages payable..	90,000	100,000
Long-term liabilities	65,000	80,000
Common stock	100,000	100,000
Retained earnings	110,000	70,000
Total liabilities and owners' equity	$400,000	$375,000

Selected information from Seaview Dairy's current year *income statement*:

Sales	$1,650,000
Cost of goods sold..	840,000
Wages expense...	260,000

a   Compute the following:

(1)   *Cash received from customers* during the year .... $_____

(2)   *Cash payments for merchandise* during the year............................. $_____

(3)   Wages *paid* to employees during the year...................................... $_____

(4)   In Seaview Dairy's statement of cash flows, what amount would be reported as the *net change in cash and cash equivalents*?

$_____ (increase/decrease)

b   Seaview Dairy recorded the sale of equipment as follows:

Cash	25,000	
Accumulated Depreciation: Equipment.......................................	20,000	
Loss on Disposal of Equipment..	15,000	
Equipment		60,000

How would this transaction be reported in Seaview Dairy's *statement of cash flows*? (Assume the direct method is being used.)

SOLUTIONS TO CHAPTER 13   10-MINUTE QUIZZES

QUIZ A
1   C
2   B
3   D
4   A

QUIZ B
1   D
2   A
3   C
4   A
5   C

QUIZ C

MANDARIN FOODS
Statement of Cash Flows
For the Year Ended December 31, 2001

Cash flows from operating activities:		
Cash received from customers...	$ 1,800,000	
Interest and dividends received..	40,000	
Cash provided by operating activities...............................		$1,840,000
Cash paid to suppliers and employees................................	$(1,400,000)	
Interest paid..	(60,000)	
Income taxes paid	(120,000)	
Cash disbursed for operating activities..............................		(1,580,000)
Net cash flow from operating activities		$ 260,000
Cash flow from investing activities:		
Cash paid to acquire land...	$ (520,000)	
Proceeds from sale of land..	50,000	
Net cash used by investing activities.................................		(470,000)
Cash flows from financing activities:		
Proceeds from issuing bonds payable.................................	$ 100,000	
Payments to settle short-term debts...................................	(70,000)	
Proceeds from issuance of stock..	400,000	
Dividends paid	(200,000)	
Net cash provided by financing activities............................		230,000
Net increase (decrease) in cash..		$ 20,000
Cash and cash equivalents, beginning of year.........................		84,000
Cash and cash equivalents, end of year		$ 104,000

QUIZ D

a

(1) $1,650,000 (sales) + $5,000 (decrease in accounts receivable) = <u>$1,655,000</u>

(2) $840,000 (cost of goods sold) - $30,000 (decrease in inventory) - $10,000 (increase in accounts payable) = <u>$800,000</u>

(3) $260,000 (wages expense) + $10,000 (decrease in wages payable) = <u>$270,000</u>

(4)   <u>$30,000</u> (Cash and cash equivalents were $110,000 at beginning of year and $140,000 at end of year.)

b   <u>$25,000</u> proceeds from disposal of equipment, classified as an investing activity *or*

<u>$25,000</u> cash provided from investing activities.

Assignment Guide to Chapter 13

	Exercises	Problems									Cases					Net
	1-11	1	2	3	4	5	6	7	8	9	1	2	3	4	5	1
Time estimate (in minutes)	<15	40	40	25	30	60	25	25	50	50	30	25	40	40	25	25
Difficulty rating	E	M	M	S	M	S	E	M	S	S	M	M	M	M	M	S
Learning Objectives:																
1. Explain the purposes and uses of a statement of cash flows.	1, 2, 11										√	√	√			
2. Describe how cash transactions are classified in a statement of cash flows.	1, 2, 7, 11	√	√					√	√	√						√
3. Compute the major cash flows relating to operating activities.	4, 5, 6		√			√		√	√	√						√
4. Compute the cash flows relating to investing and financing activities.	3, 6, 9, 11		√	√	√		√	√	√	√			√		√	√
5. Distinguish between the direct and indirect methods of reporting operating cash flows.									√	√						
6. Explain why net income differs from net cash flows from operating activities.	2, 4							√	√	√						
7. Compute net cash flows from operating activities using the *indirect method*.	9, 10						√		√	√						
8. Discuss the likely effects of various business strategies on cash flows.	8							√	√	√		√	√	√	√	
*9. Explain how a worksheet may be helpful in preparing a statement of cash flows.									√	√						

Chapter Summary

Although earlier chapters have touched on topics from financial statement analysis, we now present a comprehensive overview of the subject. The chapter is organized into three sections. We begin by introducing a number of analytical tools. Second, measures of liquidity, credit risk, and profitability are surveyed in detail. Finally, a comprehensive illustration analyzes a fictional company from the point of view of stockholders, and short and long-term creditors.

The analytical tools explained include dollar and percentage changes, trend percentages, component percentages, and ratios. Particular attention is paid to the sensitivity of percentage computations to the choice of base period. Our treatment of ratios at this point concentrates on the choice of potential standards of comparison. This first portion of the chapter concludes with an introduction to the concept of earnings quality.

The examination of measures of liquidity and credit risk begins with a definitional analysis of liquidity and the balance sheet classifications of current assets and current liabilities. With these definitions established we introduce working capital, the current ratio, the quick ratio, and debt ratio. Computation of each measure is illustrated before proceeding to show how each is used to evaluate liquidity. We identify standards for comparison and sources of data for individual companies and industries. The usefulness and limitations of these measures are explained.

A multiple-step income statement provides the foundation for profitability analysis. The gross profit rate and operating income illustrate the usefulness of income statement subtotals. Earnings per share, introduced in Chapter 12, is reexamined here and used to explain the interpretation of the price earnings ratio. Adequacy of net income is addressed via return of average assets and return on stockholders' equity.

We end the chapter with a lengthy illustration of a fictitious entity. Analysis of the example statements begins from the perspective of a stockholder. Measures examined include EPS, the p/e ratio, dividend yield, the return of assets and the return on equity. A brief discussion of the advantages of leverage precedes coverage of the debt ratio. The concerns of long-term creditors are addressed using the interest coverage ratio. The analysis by short-term creditors reprises the measures of liquidity covered earlier in the chapter. In addition, the accounts receivable turnover ratio and inventory turnover ratio are computed and interpreted. We conclude by analyzing the net cash flow from operating activities and contrasting it with net income.

Learning Objectives

1. Explain the uses of dollar and percentage changes, trend percentages, component percentages, and ratios.

2. Discuss the quality of a company's earnings, assets, and working capital.

3. Explain the nature and purpose of classifications in financial statements.

4. Prepare a classified balance sheet and compute widely used measures of liquidity and credit risk.

5. Prepare a multiple-step and single-step income statement and compute widely used measures of profitability.

6. Put a company's net income into perspective by relating it to sales, assets, and stockholders' equity.

7. Compute the ratios widely used in financial statement analysis and explain the significance of each.

8. Analyze financial statements from the viewpoints of common stockholders, creditors, and others.

Brief topical outline

    A Financial statements are designed for analysis – see *Case in Point* (page **593**)
    B Tools of analysis
        1 Dollar and percentage changes
            a Evaluating percentage changes in sales and earnings
            b Percentages become misleading when the base is small
        2 Trend percentages - see *Case in Point* (page **605**)
        3 Component percentages
        4 Ratios
        5 Standards of comparison
            a Past performance of the company
            b Industry standards
            c Quality of earnings – see *Management Strategy and Financial Reporting* (page **608**)
        6 Quality of assets and the relative amount of debt
    C Measures of liquidity and credit risk
        1 A classified balance sheet
            a Current assets
            b Current liabilities
        2 Working capital

5 Analysis by short-term creditors
    a   Amount of working capital
    b   Quality of working capital
    c   Accounts receivable turnover rate
    d   Inventory turnover rate
    e   Operating cycle
    f   Current ratio
    g   Quick ratio
    h   Unused lines of credit
6 Cash flow analysis
    a   Cash flows from operations to current liabilities
7 Usefulness of notes to financial statements - see *Your Turn* (page **637**)
F Summary of analytical measurements - see *A Second Look* (page **640**)

Topical coverage and suggested assignment

Class Meetings on Chapter	Topical Outline Coverage	Homework Assignment (To Be Completed Prior to Class)				
		Discussion Questions	Exercises	Problems	Cases	Internet
1	A – B	1, 2, 3, 4	1, 2, 3, 4	1, 2		1
2	C	9, 10, 11, 12	5, 14	3, 4, 5	2, 3	
3	D – E	17, 18, 19, 20	6, 7, 8, 9, 16	7, 8, 11	7	

Comments and observations

Teaching objectives for Chapter 14

In presenting this chapter our objectives are to:

1 Establish the usefulness of accounting information to economic decision-makers.

2 Explain the use of common analytical tools, especially percentage changes and ratios.

3 Introduce the concept of quality of earnings in financial analysis.

4 Describe the basic classifications within financial statements, and explain the usefulness of these classifications.

5 Present basic ratios used in evaluating liquidity, credit risk, and the return on invested capital.

6 Discuss the usefulness and limitations of ratio analysis.

7 Emphasize the importance of financial leverage to stockholders and creditors.

8 Present a comprehensive analysis of a set of financial statements and the notes to the statements.

New features in Chapter 14

This material has been reorganized and placed at this point in the text as a logical conclusion to the chapters on financial accounting. In all respects, the treatment of these topics in this edition parallels our earlier work.

General comments

This chapter exemplifies our continuing goal of increasing emphasis upon the *interpretation* and *use* of accounting information. Throughout the first twelve chapters we have shown not, only how accounting information is developed, but also how it is interpreted and used. We feel that it is appropriate at this point in the course to spend some amount of time concentrating on this theme.

After reviewing some straightforward analytical tools, the chapter introduces statement classifications and ratios that the student should feel comfortable studying. The illustrations involve the same merchandising business that was introduced in Chapter 5. Students have little difficulty understanding that a going-concern must be capable of satisfying its current liabilities, and that the resources to do so will come primarily from current assets. Measures such as the current and quick ratios and working capital thus have great intuitive appeal. The importance of return on investment is likewise easily motivated.

When we illustrate the usefulness of accounting information, we find those assignments based upon "name" companies particularly effective. Exercises *5, 6, 7,* and *8* and Problems *4, 5, 9,* and *13* all fall into this category.

We recommend discussing the limitations of financial ratios as well as their usefulness. For example, we discuss appropriate standards for comparison, and stress the need for the analyst to be familiar with both the company and the environment in which it operates.

An aside Class discussion of measures of solvency can be enlivened by explaining to students the nature of restrictive debt covenants. Have students visit several corporate websites and search the annual reports for restrictive debt covenants.

Supplementary Exercises

Business Week Exercise

In "IGT: A Smart Bet on Slot Machines?", *Business Week Online*, May 8, 2002, Christopher Thomas presents an update on the computer games industry in the US. IGT is the world's leading maker of slot machines, with a 60% market share. Read the article to see how the September 11 terrorist attack has hurt the casino market.

Group Exercise

Obtain the annual report of a company of your choosing. Carefully review the financial statements and then the note to the financial statements that describes the company's accounting policies. Based on your research, prepare a report explaining areas of concern over the quality of the company's reported earnings.

Internet Exercise

Choose five well-known corporations. From the site www.pcquote.com obtain an analysis of the stock price performance of the companies chosen since 2000. Suppose you had invested $1,000 in each of these companies on January 1, 2000. Calculate the value of this $5,000 portfolio at present.

Indicate the best answer to each question in the space provided.

_____ 1 The quick ratio is considered more useful than the current ratio for:
a Evaluating the profitability of a business that sells inventory very quickly, such as a restaurant.
b Evaluating the solvency of a business that turns inventory into cash very slowly, such as a shipbuilder.
c Evaluating long-term credit risk.
d Evaluating investors' expectations concerning future earnings.

_____ 2 The debt ratio is a measure of:
a Net cash flows relating to financing activities.
b Long-term credit risk.
c Short-term solvency.
d Profitability, independent of the manner in which assets are financed.

_____ 3 In the long-run, it is most important for a business to generate an inflow of cash from its:
a Operating activities.
b Stockholders.
c Investing activities.
d Creditors.

_____ 4 Return on assets measures the efficiency with which management:
a Generates earnings from the assets under its control, regardless of how these assets are financed.
b Generates earnings from the assets under its control, giving consideration to any costs of financing these assets.
c Generates cash from the assets under its control, regardless of accrual-based measures of profitability.
d Converts its current assets into cash.

_____ 5 A transaction that will increase the quick ratio but cause the current ratio to decline is:
a Short-term borrowing.
b Investing cash in plant assets.
c Sale of inventory at a price below cost.
d Collection of an account receivable.

Based upon the below information, indicate the best answer in the space provided.

Shown below are data taken from a recent annual report of ***Reebok International Ltd.*** (Dollar amounts in millions.)

	Beginning of Year	End of Year
Balance sheet data:		
Current assets..	$ 714	$ 784
Total assets...	1,063	1,166
Current liabilities..	256	203
Total liabilities...	372	322
Total stockholders' equity.....................................	691	844
Income statement data:		
Net sales		1,822
Gross profit..		750
Operating income..		293
Net income..		175

_____ 1 The current ratio at year-end (rounded to the nearest tenth) is:
    a   2.4 to 1.   **c**   3.9 to 1.
    b   .7 to 1.   **d**   Some other answer.

_____ 2 The amount of working capital at the ***beginning*** of the year (in millions) was:
    a $581.   **c** $342.
    b $691.   **d**   Some other answer.

_____ 3 The gross profit rate for the year (rounded to the nearest 1 percent) was:
    a   41%.   **c**   64%.
    b   59%.   **d**   Some other answer

_____ 4 The return on average total assets during the year (rounded to the nearest percent) was:
    a   16%.   **c**   67%.
    b   26%.   **d**   Some other answer.

_____ 5 The return on average total stockholders' equity during the year (rounded to the nearest 1 percent) was:
    a   98%.   **c**   23%.
    b   38%.   **d**   Some other answer.

Based on the information below, computer the following:

Shown below are data taken from a recent annual report of Bevar, Inc. (Dollar amounts in millions.)

	Beginning of Year	End of Year
Balance sheet data:		
Current assets..	$ 600	$ 650
Total assets..	1,000	1,200
Current liabilities...	250	200
Total liabilities...	450	500
Total stockholders' equity................................	550	700
Income statement data:		
Net sales		1,600
Gross profit..		600
Operating income...		200
Net income		150

a   Current ratio at *year-end* (round to nearest tenth).   _____ to 1

b   Working capital at the *beginning* of the year
    (in millions) $_____

c   Gross profit rate for the year (round to the
    nearest 1 percent)   _____%

d   Return on average total assets for the year
    (round to the nearest 1 percent)   _____%

e   Return on average total equity for the year
    (round to the nearest 1 percent)   _____%

Given below are comparative balance sheets and an income statement for the Dyson Corporation:

Dyson Corporation Balance Sheets – Current Year	Dec. 31	Jan. 1
Cash	$ 27,000	$ 23,000
Accounts receivable	215,000	185,000
Inventory	148,000	152,000
Equipment (net)	110,000	130,000
	$500,000	$490,000
Accounts payable	115,000	126,000
Dividends payable	15,000	12,000
Capital stock, $10 par	100,000	100,000
Retained earnings	270,000	252,000
	$500,000	$490,000

Dyson Corporation Income Statement for the Current Year	
Sales	$900,000
Cost of goods sold	(540,000)
Gross profit on sales	$360,000
Operating expenses	(261,000)
Operating income	$ 99,000
Interest expense and income taxes	(23,200)
Net income	$ 75,800

All sales were made on account. Cash dividends declared during the year totaled $57,800. Compute the following:

a   Average accounts receivable turnover   _____times

b   Book value per share at the end of the current year $_____

c   Earnings per share of capital stock $_____

d   Return on assets   _____ %

e   Return on common stockholders' equity is computed by dividing $_____ by $_____

SOLUTIONS TO CHAPTER 14   10-MINUTE QUIZZES

QUIZ A		QUIZ B	
1	B	1	C
2	B	2	D ($714 - $256 = $458)
3	A	3	A
4	A	4	B
5	C	5	C

QUIZ C

a   Current ratio at year-end   <u>3.25 to 1</u>
$650 ÷ $200 = 3.25

b   Working capital at the *beginning* of the year (in millions)   <u>$350</u>
$600 - $250 = $350

c   Gross profit rate   <u>37.5%</u>
$600 ÷ $1,600 = 37.5%

d   Return on average total assets   <u>18.2%</u>
$200 ÷ [($1,000 + $1,200) ÷ 2] = 18.2%

e   Return on average total stockholders' equity   <u>24%</u>
$150 ÷ [($550 + $700) ÷ 2] = 24%

QUIZ D

1   Accounts receivable turnover ($900,000 ÷ $200,000) = <u>4.5 times</u>
2   Book value per share at the end of the current year = ($370,000 ÷ 10,000 shares) = <u>$37.00</u>
3   Earnings per share of capital stock ($75,800 ÷ 10,000 shares) = <u>$7.58</u>
4   Return on assets ($99,000/$495,000) = <u>20%</u>
5   Return on common stockholders' equity is computed by dividing $75,800 by $361,000.
$361,000 = [($370,000 + $352,000) ÷ 2]

Assignment Guide to Chapter 14

Learning Objectives	Exercises	P1	P2	P3	P4	P5	P6	P7	P8	P9	P10	P11	P12	P13	C1	C2	C3	C4	C5	C6	C7	Net
Time estimate (in minutes)	<15	30	30	25	30	25	30	60	60	35	35	35	30	60	40	40	40	40	40	40	40	30
Difficulty rating	E	M	M	E	M	E	M	S	S	M	M	M	M	S	M	M	S	M	M	S	M	M
1. Explain the uses of dollar and percentage changes, trend percentages, component percentages, and ratios.	1, 2, 3, 4, 9	√													√						√	
2. Discuss the quality of a company's earnings, assets, and working capital.	4																				√	
3. Explain the nature and purpose of classifications in financial statements.	4, 5, 11		√	√	√	√																
4. Prepare a classified balance sheet and compute widely used measures of liquidity and credit risk.	4, 5, 11, 12			√	√	√	√	√	√	√			√				√					
5. Prepare a multiple-step and a single-step income statement and compute widely used measures of profitability.	4, 6	√	√				√	√	√	√	√	√	√	√		√						
6. Put a company's net income into perspective by relating it to sales, assets, and stockholders' equity.	4, 7, 8, 9, 10, 11, 12												√			√						
7. Compute the ratios widely used in financial statement analysis and explain the significance of each.	4, 13, 14, 15, 16				√			√	√	√	√	√	√	√		√		√	√	√		√
8. Analyze financial statements from the viewpoints of common stockholders, creditors, and others.												√						√	√	√		√

Chapter Summary

The chapter focuses on some of the aspects of the global environment that have an impact on accounting. We begin with a brief introduction to the process of globalization of a business. Globalization is presented as a continuous process whereby managers become aware of the impact of international activities on their companies. This process takes place in stages that include exporting, licensing joint ventures, wholly owned subsidiaries, and global sourcing. Each stage has implications for the type of accounting information reported.

The process of globalization is shaped by environmental forces including political and legal systems, economic systems, culture, and technology and infrastructure. Each of these factors is shown to have an impact on accounting information. For example, planned economic systems require very different forms of financial reporting than market economies.

Numerous accounting problems follow from the use of multiple currencies in carrying out transactions internationally. The chapter introduces exchange rates and exchange rate computations. We then illustrate journal entries to account for a number of credit transactions with foreign companies. These include explanations of the source of gains and losses on fluctuations in foreign currency. We also demonstrate the adjustment of foreign receivables and payables at the balance sheet date. This section of the chapter closes with a brief discussion of hedging strategies to avoid losses due to currency fluctuations.

The chapter concludes with a brief discussion of global sourcing and the Foreign Corrupt Practices Act. The FCPA is shown to have important implications for record keeping and internal control in companies engaged in global sourcing.

Learning Objectives

1.   Define four mechanisms companies use to globalize their business activities.

2.   Identify how global environmental forces – a) political and legal systems, b) economic systems, c) culture, and d) technology and infrastructure – affect financial reporting practices.

3.   Explain why there is demand for harmonization of global financial reporting standards.

4.   Demonstrate how to convert an amount of money from one currency to another.

5. Compute gains or losses on receivables or payables that are stated in a foreign currency when exchange rates fluctuate.

6. Describe several techniques for "hedging" against losses from fluctuations in exchange rates.

7. Understand how global sourcing increases product cost complexity.

8. Explain the importance of the Foreign Corrupt Practices Act.

Brief topical outline

A Globalization - see *Case in Point* (page **672**)
B Environmental forces shaping globalization
   1   Political and legal systems – see *Case in Point* (page **673**)
   2   Economic systems - see *Case in Point* (page **674**)
   3   Culture – see *Case in Point* (pg **675**), *Management Strategy* (pg **676**)
   3   Technology and infrastructure - see *Case in Point* (pages **676-77**)
C Harmonization of financial reporting standards – see *Case in Point* (pg **678**)
D Foreign currencies and exchange rates
   1   Exchange rates
      a   Exchange rate jargon
   2   Accounting for transactions with foreign companies
      a   Credit purchases with prices stated in a foreign currency
      b Credit sales with prices stated in a foreign currency – see *Case in Point* (page **682**)
      c   Adjustment of foreign receivables and payables at the balance sheet date – see *Cash Effects* (page **684**)
   3   Currency fluctuations –who wins and who loses?
      a   Strategies to avoid losses from rate fluctuations
      b   Hedging – see *Case in Point* (page **685**)
      c   Exchange rates and competitive prices – see *Your Turn* (page **686**)
   4   Consolidated financial statements that include foreign subsidiaries
E Global sourcing
   1   Foreign Corrupt Practices Act – see *Your Turn* (p **689**), *A Second Look* (p **690**)

Topical coverage and suggested assignment

Class Meetings on Chapter	Topical Outline Coverage	Homework Assignment (To Be Completed Prior to Class)				
		Discussion Questions	Exercises	Problems	Cases	Internet
1	A – C	1, 2, 10, 11	1, 2, 3	7	1	1
2	D – E	3, 4, 6, 7, 8, 13	5, 6, 8	1, 2, 3		

Comments and observations

Teaching objectives for Chapter 15

In presenting this material objectives are to:

1   Define the process of globalization.

2   Provide a number of examples of the impact of the global environment on how accounting information is gathered and reported.

3   Explain the computations necessary to convert an amount from one currency to another.

4   Distinguish between rising and falling exchange rates.

5   Explain the sources of gains and losses form exchange rate fluctuations and illustrate the journal entries to record these gains and losses.

6   Review the provisions of the Foreign Corrupt Practices Act that have an impact on accounting and systems of internal control

New features in Chapter 15

With the exception of the material on exchange rates, which was included as an appendix in our prior edition, this chapter is entirely new to the eleventh edition.

General comments

The accelerating pace of globalization in business has made it incumbent upon us to introduce students to some of the accounting issues surrounding the phenomenon. If accounting is the language of business then like any language it will reflect the environment in which it is developed and used. The diversity in accounting worldwide is a logical extension of the variety of business environments throughout the world. The text identifies a small subset of environmental factors as being highly influential on the evolution of accounting. The economic and legal system, culture, and existing technology and infrastructure have a powerful effect on the relationship between businesses and the providers of capital. This relationship in turn determines the type of accounting information that the environment will demand. In making this argument we particularly like using Exercise *4* and Case *2*. The former requires some straightforward research into the environmental factors identified as crucial to the success of globalization strategies, while the case requires students to develop arguments that hinge on the relationship between accounting standards and the environment.

Although the more complex accounting issues surrounding foreign currency transactions are not appropriate for the first course, we believe that all students should have a fundamental understanding of the use of exchange rates and currency conversions. Once they have mastered the basic arithmetic of converting amounts from one currency to another, it is relatively simple to demonstrate the potential gains and losses from credit transactions denominated in the foreign currency. To this end, we highly recommend reviewing Problems *2* and *3*. These problems provide the opportunity to introduce hedging strategies to avoid losses on such transactions. We highly recommend class discussion of hedging, since this will provide one of the few opportunities in the course to at least touch on the nature of derivative securities.

Supplemental Exercises

Business Week Exercise

In "Can the SEC Make Foreign Companies Play By Its Rules?", *Business Week*, March 6, 2000, Mike McNamee discusses why the International Accounting Standard Committee's accounting standards are less rigorous than those of the SEC. After reading the article, report on how European and Asian companies wanting to trade their stocks in US markets without adopting US GAAP could hurt investors.

Group Exercise

In "Corporate Standards: Raise the Bar Around the World", *Business Week*, May 13, 2002, Jeffrey Garten argues that the US Securities & Exchange Commission should embrace international accounting standards. He discusses the need for improvement of assets and the importance of establishing national standards relating to the qualifications and responsibilities of boards of directors. After reading the article, evaluation the suggestion that American stock exchanges should work with European and Asian exchanges to press for higher governance, and that financial institutions develop metrics to evaluate corporate governance.

Internet Exercise

The International Accounting Standards Board maintains a website at http://www.iasc.org.uk/cmt/0001.asp. Visit the site and browse to see what information you can gather. Check the current projects that the board is considering and write a brief report concerning the proposal.

Indicate the best answer for each question in the space provided.

Use the following data for questions 1 through 3.

Mandy Winger owns an American Company that sells music cassettes to Mexican outlets. On December 10, 2000, she sold tapes to Melody of Mexico for a price of 12,500 pesos, due in 60 days. The foreign currency exchange rates on specific dates are as follows:

Dec. 10, 2000	$.1600 per peso
Dec. 31, 2000	$.1344 per peso
Feb. 8, 2001	$.1536 per peso

_____ 1   ***Refer to the above data.*** The journal entry to record the sale in Winger's accounting records on ***December 10, 2000***, includes:
  a   A debit to Accounts Receivable for 12,500 pesos.
  b   A credit to Sales for $2,000.
  c   A debit to Loss on Fluctuation of Foreign Currency for $250.
  d   No entry is made until year-end on this type of transaction..

_____ 2   ***Refer to the above data.*** With regard to this transaction, Winger's financial statements at ***December 31, 2000***, include:
  a   An account receivable of $2,000
  b   A gain on fluctuation of foreign currency of $320
  c   Sales revenue of $1,680
  d   A loss on fluctuation of foreign currency of $320.

_____ 3   ***Refer to the above data.*** Which of the following is ***not*** true regarding the above sales transaction to Melody of Mexico?
  a   Winger recognizes a loss on fluctuation of foreign currency in the amount of $80 in 2001.
  b   Winger recognizes a gain on fluctuation of foreign currency in the amount of $240 in 2001.
  c   Winger has incurred an overall loss of $80 on fluctuation of foreign currency in the period from December 10, 2000 to February 8, 2001.
  d   Winger could have avoided any loss due to fluctuations in foreign currency by setting the sales price of the cassettes in terms of U.S. dollars instead of pesos.

_____ 4   Which of the following businesses or individuals would benefit most from a strong U.S. dollar?
  a   A small store that sells American-made cameras in St. Louis, Missouri. The store has no foreign receivables or payables.
  b   The Cancun, Mexico, outlet for Levi's jeans (made in the U.S.)
  c   International Harvester (an American manufacturer of farming machinery that sells equipment to foreign customers.)
  d   An American tourist visiting France.

CHAPTER 15   NAME_____ #_____

10-MINUTE QUIZ B   SECTION_____

Omaha Ranchers exports beef to Japan. In the space provided below, prepare journal entries to record the following events.

2000

Nov. 1   Sold beef steaks to a Japanese restaurant chain at a price of 1 million yen, due in 90 days. The current exchange rate is .0100 US dollars per yen. (Omaha uses the periodic inventory method.)

Dec. 31   Omaha made a year-end adjusting entry relating to the account receivable from the Japanese restaurant chain. The exchange rate at year-end is .0102 US dollars per yen.

2001

Feb. 1   Received a check for $10,100 from the InterContinental Bank in full settlement of the receivable from the Japanese restaurant chain. The exchange rate at this date is .0101 US dollars per yen.

2000	General Journal		
Nov. 1			
Dec. 31			
2001			
Feb. 1			

CHAPTER 15   NAME_____ #_____

10-MINUTE QUIZ C   SECTION_____

The following table summarizes the facts of five independent cases (labeled *a* through *e*) of American companies engaging in credit transactions with foreign corporations while the foreign exchange rate is fluctuating:

| Case | **Column** | | | |
	Type of Credit Transaction 1	Currency Used in Contract 2	Exchange Rate Direction 3	Effect on Income 4
a	Sales	Foreign currency	Falling	
b	Purchases		Falling	No effect
c	Purchases	Foreign currency		Gain
d	Sales	U.S. dollars	Rising	
e		Foreign currency	Rising	Loss

Instructions

Notice that for each case, a blank space has been left in one of the four columns. You are to fill this blank space after evaluating the information about the case provided in the other three columns. The content of each column and the word or words that you should enter in the blank spaces are described below:

Column 1 indicates the type of credit transaction in which the American company engaged with the foreign corporations. The answer entered in this column should be either *"Sales"* or *"Purchases."*

Column 2 indicates the currency in which the invoice price is stated. The answer may be either *"U.S. dollars"* or *"Foreign currency."*

Column 3 indicates the direction in which the foreign currency exchange rate has moved between the date of the credit transaction and the date of settlement. The answer in this column may be either *"Rising"* or *"Falling."*

Column 4 indicates the effect of the exchange rate fluctuation upon the income of the American company. The answers entered in this column are to be selected from the following: *"Gain," "Loss,"* or *"No effect.*

Listed below are nine global business terms introduced in this chapter:

Foreign exchange risk	*Future contracts*	*International Accounting Standards Board*
Loss on fluctuation in Foreign exchange rates	*Hedging*	*Exporting*
Planned economy	*International licensing*	*Foreign Corrupt Practices Act*

Each of the following statements may (or may not) describe one of these terms. In the space provided below each statement, indicate the accounting term described, or answer None if the statement does not correctly describe any of the terms

a   The strategy of creating offsetting positions so that losses from currency fluctuations will be offset by gains resulting from the same fluctuations.

_____

b   Selling a good or service to a foreign customer.

_____

c   Government allocates resources and determines output through central planning

_____

d   The organization responsible for developing uniform worldwide accounting standards.

_____

e   Distinguishes between illegal influence peddling and legal facilitating payments.

_____

f   A cross-border contractual agreement allowing one company to use trademarks, patents or technology of another company.

_____

g   The impact on the value of a company of unexpected fluctuations in the exchange rate.

_____

SOLUTIONS TO CHAPTER 15 10-MINUTE QUIZZES

QUIZ A
1 B
2 D
3 A
4 D

QUIZ B

2000	General Journal		
Nov. 1	Accounts receivable	10,000	
	Sales		10,000
	To record the sale of beef steaks to Japanese restaurant for		
	1 million yen when the exchange rate is 0.0100 US dollars per		
	yen. (1 million yen X 0.0100 = $10,000)		
Dec. 31	Accounts receivable	200	
	Gain on fluctuations in foreign exchange rates		200
	To adjust balance of 10,000 dollar accounts receivable to amount		
	indicated by year-end exchange rate:		
	Original account balance $10,000		
	Adjusted balance (1 million yen X 0.0102) 10,200		
	Required adjustment (gain) $ 200		
2001			
Feb. 1	Cash	10,100	
	Loss on fluctuations in foreign exchange rate	100	
	Accounts receivable		10,200
	To record receipt of $10,100 in settlement of account receivable,		
	and to recognize loss from fall in exchange rate since Dec. 31.		
	Accounts receivable, adjusted balance $10,200		
	Amount paid, February 1 10,100		
	Loss from decline in exchange rate $ 100		

QUIZ C

Case	Column			
	Type of Credit Transaction 1	Currency Used in Contract 2	Exchange Rate Direction 3	Effect on Income 4
a	Sales	Foreign currency	Falling	Loss
b	Purchases	U.S. dollars	Falling	No effect
c	Purchases	Foreign currency	Falling	Gain
d	Sales	U.S. dollars	Rising	No effect
e	Purchases	Foreign currency	Rising	Loss

QUIZ D

a Hedging
b Exporting
c Planned economy
d International Accounting Standards Board
e Foreign Corrupt Practices Act
f International licensing
g Foreign exchange risk

Assignment Guide to Chapter 15

Learning Objectives:	Exercises 1-8	P1	P2	P3	P4	P5	P6	P7	C1	C2	C3	Net 1
Time estimate (in minutes)	<15	40	40	25	30	60	25	25	30	30	30	25
Difficulty rating	E	M	M	M	S	M	S	E	M	M	M	M
1. Define four mechanisms companies use to globalize their business activities.	1, 2											√
2. Identify how global environmental forces – (a) political and legal systems, (b) economic systems, (c) culture, and (d) technology and infrastructure – affect financial reporting practices.	1, 2, 3, 4, 5,					√		√	√		√	√
3. Explain why there is demand for harmonization of global financial reporting standards.	1, 7			√	√		√	√	√	√	√	
4. Demonstrate how to convert an amount of money from one currency to another.	1, 6,	√	√	√	√		√					
5. Compute gains or losses on receivables or payables that are stated in a foreign currency when exchange rates fluctuate.	1, 5, 6	√	√	√			√	√		√		
6. Describe several techniques for "hedging" against losses from fluctuations in exchange rates.	1		√	√		√	√	√				
7. Understand how global sourcing increases product cost complexity.	1, 3, 4,		√	√		√		√				√
8. Explain the importance of the Foreign Corrupt Practices Act.	1, 4, 8											

©The McGraw-Hill Companies, Inc., 2003
Instructor's Resource Manual